TIP—TOP
SECRET

10987654321 Library of Congress
Cataloging in Publication Data
        Lyne, William R.
        Occult Ether Physics
        I. Title
PS: 93-90554
ISBN: 0-9637467-6-6

Non-fiction: A re-discovery of what the author calls "occult ether physics", the scientific/technical basis for a space-propulsion system invented in the late 19th century by Nikola Tesla, now used in the secret, exclusively man-made flying machines known as "flying saucers" or "UFOs". The government conceals this invention behind false scientific theories, "space alien" hoaxes, and false propaganda, disseminated through a controlled mass media. A "UFOlogy", "new-age", "paranormalist", and "pseudo-debunker" network is criminally maintained under "national security laws", to blur the facts of reality and disjoint inquiry, thus protecting the archaic technology and resources of coercive-monopolist, corporate-state interests from the competition of a truly free market.

OCCULT ETHER PHYSICS:

TESLA'S HIDDEN SPACE PROPULSION SYSTEM AND THE CONSPIRACY TO CONCEAL IT

By
William Lyne

The truth can flow from lies, but lies cannot flow from the truth.

Arthur Schopenhauer

TABLE OF CONTENTS

PREFACE

There is much consternation today about the words "cult" and "occult", and what they mean. Many are worried that their own organizations, groups, or religions may fall into this category. Since the word "occult" merely refers to "secret" or "hidden", it is used by doctors to describe unknown bacteria as being "occult". As for a religion, philosophy, organization or other group activity, it is a "cult" if it utilizes "secret teachings", made known only to a select few initiates or "priests".

Is it possible that an entire area of physics has been declared virtually "occult" and "off-limits" to the public or to private individuals, by a powerful group, so that all science education or data generally available to the public has been "screened" to eliminate references to it? Is it possible that the actual science involved in "electro-propulsion", has been replaced with a "bogus science", which has been promoted and promulgated to the extent that no one except the 'esoteric elite' knows the truth? And if so, has the "occult" science become the exclusive province of a very few specially selected corporate/government "priests"?

I began studying this controversy---including the science involved--- when I was but a child of eight years, in 1946, after interviewing oil field pumpers who had seen silvery "flying disks" in the remote oil fields in the west Texas and southern New Mexico desert. At the age of 13, I spent a couple of days visiting with family friends and their neighbor, astrophysicist Dr. Lincoln La Paz, in Albuquerque, New Mexico. La Paz was then employed by the U.S. government to help cover up Nazi flying saucer technology brought to New Mexico after WWII. My early convictions were later corroborated when I acquired a piece of hardware from a 1943 German flying saucer at Sandia Base where La Paz worked.

Since the truth about electropropulsion is based on "ether" (A.K.A. "aether") physics, which has been collected, hidden away, or declared "national security secrets", or intentionally obliterated by false propaganda which is so intense that the general public remains unaware of the facts which are right under their noses, I have dubbed the ether physics ultimately connected to electro-propulsion, "Occult Ether Physics". This book is dedicated to the rediscovery of, examination of, and the integration of these secrets into the public knowledge.

The high priests of this occult knowledge are the elite owners of the coercive monopolist corporate banking, industrial, mineral and related interests, who in turn allow the initiation of certain scientists, military and

1

government officials into their secret teachings only insofar as it is necessary, to execute and maintain a conspiracy of giant proportions, so that the technology can be classified as a "state secret" which can be controlled and enforced by means of unconstitutional "national security laws", military and civilian legal authority, and police. These measures are intended to protect the archaic technology and resources controlled by the élite, from the competition of a truly free market society.

Because of the last 76 or more years of progressively intensifying false propaganda and manipulation of knowledge and science, a majority of scientists ridicule the concepts of the existence of an ether and of flying saucers, as if such thinking belonged in the category of a "flat earth" theory and the "little green men" from outer space babblings, but the reverse is true. The proponents of Relativism and the *Big Bang* (the "Big Bangers") want you to believe that the universe is finite, so that, if you go "too far", you will "fall off the universe", rather than off a "flat earth". What's the difference? Flat earth...finite universe...they're both dumb theories.

And what do the "little green men" lies have to do with exclusively man-made electric flying machines, and technology based on sound and well-established electrical science and physics, but which, like the existence of the ether, has been tucked away in secret vaults, to keep you from using it, while you are being fed false and useless "theories"? These range from "curved space", "time travel", "Big Bang", and "alien abduction" stories, to "parallel universe", "interdimensional travel", and any other outrageously incredible stories, concocted by government spooks, national security personnel, and secret agents in the "UFOlogy" and "pseudo-debunker" communities ("pseudo-debunkers" in my vernacular, are official government spokesmen or scientific know-it-alls whose job it is to completely deny the existence of flying saucers, or to ridicule their other covert government counterparts, the UFOlogists, new-agers, or paranormalists).

Before you decide there is no ether, or no flying saucers, or before you believe the often-told "prime-time" lies that aliens are "here", or that time-travel is possible, you should ask yourself whether or not your thinking on these subjects has been conditioned by Big Brother's Biggest Lies. If you believe in relativism, I should point out that "time- travel" is an integral part of that, which is a very incredible impossibility which makes the so-called "science" you rely on a worthless piece of pseudo-intellectual crap concocted by someone who wanted to sabotage your mind

2

on behalf of the self-appointed high priests of "Occult Ether Physics".

Is your thinking a barometer of thought-control mediocrity? Are you so out of control of your own metaphysical concepts and epistemology, that you have to get your thinking from the "canned goods" section of NASA (NAZIA), courtesy of the CIA's *Office of Scientific Intelligence* ("OSI")? Is your education a TV dinner, prepared by a Secret Government, so you'll never discover the real food for thought?

For those of you who may be unfamiliar with my more complete exposition of the whys, wherefores, whos, and other facts concerning the huge volume of false propaganda designed and disseminated on behalf of the coercive monopolist corporate state, to conceal flying saucer electropropulsion and other advanced and "free energy" technology, you should read my prior book, *Space Aliens From the Pentagon*, copyright Wm. R. Lyne, 1993, ISBN 0-9637467-0-7; 1995 2nd ed., ISBN 0-9637467-1-5; 1999 3rd revised ed., ISBN 0-9637467-7-4.

The flying saucer is a product of Nikola Tesla's life work, his most fundamentally important invention, for which all his other inventions were in pursuit of, though you probably have never heard this fact from anyone else. How do I know? I have documented it in many years of research, tracing Tesla's developments and his own words uttered and published during his lifetime, in scattered, sparse yet sufficient sources, as he placed a crowning achievement on top the work of the world's greatest scientific minds of the nineteenth century, who were Tesla's inspirations.

It was supposedly proved, on May 29, 1919, "...that we live in a curved four-dimensional space-time". Albert Einstein said a massive body spinning in space "...would drag space and time around with it...", the origin of so-called "frame-dragging" and "space curvature". "Gravity is no longer a mysterious force acting at a distance but the result of an object trying to travel in a straight line through space curved by the presence of material bodies" (Gary Taubes, *Relativists in Orbit*, <u>Discover</u>, March, 1997).

Even such theories...Relativistic bromides interlaced with such phrases as "the 'fabric' of 'space-time'", "space curvature", and "frame-dragging", although off-the-wall flaky, suggest the existence of an ether, albeit an erroneous concept of the ether.

Since 1919, Nikola Tesla's electropropulsive discoveries have been concealed by government suppression, theft, and ridicule, while "science" has become a pseudo-scientific mathematical shell-game which bears little new fruit, and less resemblance to reality. It is time for the truth.

INTRODUCTION: NIKOLA TESLA'S ORIGINAL 1875 PLAN

Tesla's original vision, in his 1870's student days, of his "ideal flying machine", was of an electropulsive one, the realization of which is why he said he originally entered the field of electrical science in 1875 in the first place. This was the problem which he had assigned to himself as his main lifelong work. (Frank Parker Stockbridge, *The Tesla Turbine*, <u>The World's Work</u>, march, 1912, pp. 543-48.)

Originally anticipating that the electrical power needs for an electropropulsive craft would be too great for an on-board power plant (since his ship was to be devoid of sustaining planes), he initially embarked on developing his "wireless transmission of power" system, so as to transmit the anticipated power needed from ground-based power generators and stations. Some of these earlier Tesla ideas turned out to be unnecessary for his flying machine, so he turned them for intended commercial purposes. Since his conception of the ether was of a relatively low-density one, and his conception of the electromagnetic force not nearly so much stronger than the gravitational one, his later discovery that his prior anticipation of greater electrical power needs than actually required, led to changes in his electropropulsive craft, and produced plenty of surplus "spin-off" technology.

During the 1920's, at a time when he was in great need of money to complete his electropropulsive ship, he unsuccessfully attempted to interest the U.S. government in some of this surplus "spin off" technology. In an unpublished article prepared but never published, Tesla said: "...we should push the development of flying machines and wireless transmission of energy without an instant's delay and with all the power and resources of the nation". The immediate association here is between "flying machines" (not "aeroplanes") and "wireless transmission of energy". Tesla had piles of patents which produced him no money, because the Morgans and Rockefellers had declared them off limits. No one could borrow money from the banks to put one of these systems into practice, and anyone who was foolish enough to do so on their own money could expect the wrath of the gods to come down on them like lightening bolts from Zeus.

Due to his imminent discovery that his on-board power needs would not be so great, and a failure to interest anyone in the development of his wireless energy transmission system, Tesla obtained a patent in 1913 on a remarkable turbine he had invented about 1909. This was probably in view of encouraging developments and awareness which showed that the

4

electromagnetic interaction is 10^{40} times stronger than the gravitational interaction (George Gamow, *Gravity*, Anchor Books, N.Y. [1962], p. 138). According to Hendrick Lorenz, the electrical attractive force is 2×10^{39} times stronger than the gravitational attractive force.

The change in Tesla's strategy seems to have occurred between his 1915 test of an electropropulsive missile using wireless energy projected to it by a power beam from the ground, and his 1934 birthday announcement. These new developments were probably spurred on by the mother of invention, since without a wireless energy system, the prior conception would be rather useless. The power monopolists could fight that off forever, so Tesla was left to his own devices, unable to count on anyone else.

The earlier misconceptions were still somewhat in Tesla's mind when he developed the turbine commercially under the Tesla Propulsion Company slogan, "20 Horsepower Per Pound", with the undisclosed intention of also using the turbine to drive one of his specially designed high frequency alternators to power the ship. After having developed such a light and powerful turbine, which could turn upwards of 30,000 rpm., with a twenty pound unit producing over 200 brake horsepower on gasoline, he also designed and received a patent in 1928 for a new kind of "VTOL"-type propellor-driven airplane, to be powered by two turbines mounted in tandem, which would counteract the torque of the prop, and eliminate the need for the stabilizing props that helicoptors have on their back fuselages. This aircraft, if built, would have had a superior weight-to-horsepower ratio---perhaps three-to-one---and would have been very fast in level flight, taking off vertically.

Tesla, on seeing the innefficient use of heavier aircraft engines then in use, and the requirements of more cumbersome aircraft with greater wing area, apparently wished to commercialize on the turbine by designing and patenting the new airplane, which specifically used his turbine, to raise needed capital to complete his more expensive electropropulsive project. In his experiences with prior patents, he had learned that a patent would be worthless unless he could get the needed capital to carry the project out before the patent period expired, and that the disclosure in a patent would allow others to do so only 17 years after a patent might be granted to him, during which time his invention could languish for lack of funding on his part, because the monolithic financial interests were set against him.

While in the initial stages of development, Tesla seemed quite unaware of the true power of "the force", until his early field tests of 1915 proved that it was "tremendous". In the years 1893 and 1894, Tesla had "completely worked out" his *Dynamic Theory of Gravity*, that is, at least in "theory". Inherent to that theory, was his electropropulsion system, yet in the formative and theoretical stages. To publish his theory however, would have been tantamount to disclosing the basic technology as well, which would have allowed his competitors with the money and resources, to complete and take credit for the most important work of Tesla's life, and the greatest invention of mankind. Tesla lacked the necessary money, and could not raise it. He could not protect himself by patent, until he completed and tested a working model of large enough scale to impress the aircraft industry and the government. Fatefully, it was during this time of greatest financial need, when he still had the physical stamina to carry the project out, that he was run ragged by bill collections and foreclosures, at the behest of J.P. Morgan and his cohorts, all with the intent of crushing Tesla because he kept coming up with new electric power systems which made his prior systems obsolete. Since the systems would have ruined Morgan and Rockefeller, and since any invention which Tesla marketed for great profit would have allowed him the resources to build his energy systems, he had to be crushed. Tesla never seemed to fully realize that Morgan's pseudo-philantropism was nothing more than a scheme to compromise Tesla's contract with himself, and a way of falsely inducing Tesla's reliance on others rather than on his own self-reliance. This treatment set Tesla back emotionally as well as financially and technically, and reduced him at one point to a heap of groveling nerves, literally begging Morgan to make good on his promises, to no avail, but like all truly tragic figures, there was a *peripides*---a reassertion of the tragic hero's excellent and untarnished Arturian powers---before he passed heroically into the oblivion of death, as his discoveries, like the sword *Excalibur*, sank beneath the waters of the lake of 'national security' lies, to the inurement of corporate greed, coercion and extortion.

The only power that Tesla seemed to have left, was that of withholding his discoveries from the world, to protect his secrets from the pilfering paws of the looters, unless he could receive the compensation and credit which he deserved, but that didn't matter, because they got it all before his corpse was cool, and never paid him so much as a dime for his trouble.

After becoming aware of the true power of "the force"---one hundred billion thousand trillion thousand trillion times stronger than gravity---Tesla began to pursue the idea of an "on-board" power system for a manned craft to be used for transportation, with his "wireless transmission of power" to be relegated to a robotic, remote controlled, electropropulsive "missile", for use in warfare, with electric power to be transmitted to missiles from the ground. After a long period of silence following his field testing of a working model of the electrically propelled missile in 1915, Tesla began referring to the propelling force as "tremendous" in his later announcements which began in the '30's. "Tremendous" does not mean something which reacts feebly, to barely get off the ground, but to something which rises with great and astounding force, such as the way I saw a flying saucer perform in 1953...only ten years after Tesla's death. If "tremendous" meant something like an airplane or conventional rocket---as the CIA/NASA misinformationists have idiotically attempted to misconstrue---then what would be the word to describe a force which propels a flying saucer at 9,000 mph in three seconds?

The words "means of propulsion", used by Tesla in his 1940 interview with William L. Laurence of the *New York Times,* are of the utmost importance for those interested in understanding both the misinformational conspiracy, as well as the scanty documentation of Tesla's concealed discoveries. In their context, these words denoted an on-board electropropulsive means to be used on his "ideal" flying machine, either manned or unmanned, controlled "mechanically" by a pilot on board, or "remotely by wireless energy" by a controller from the ground. It did not refer to a "projectile" such as a "pellet" or "bullet", which had no "propulsion system", and was merely "repelled" by a gun of some sort, and it did not refer to any kind of "airplane"---hence "flying machine"---since his machine was to have no wings, ailerons, propellors, or outer appurtenances of any kind. "Propulsion" here means an on-board system for perpetuation of motion, by electromagnetic means, supplied with electrical power by either on-board generator, or by electrical energy and control signals transmitted by power beam from the ground. The idea of interplanetary travel appealed to Tesla, with the idea that, so long as the electrical energy for propulsion could be transmitted from the earth, a space ship would require no fuel tanks.

In a letter to his friend and financial supporter B.A. Behrend in the 1930's, Tesla referred cryptically to his electropropulsive discovery: "What I shall accomplish by that other invention I came specially to see you about, I do not dare to tell you. This is stated in all seriousness." Tesla apparently was inferring a plan to discover "other worlds" in outer space with his electrical machines.

Tesla realized that all solid bodies contain "electrical content", and that they behave as resonant cavities, which interact electromagnetically with rapidly varying electrostatic forces and ether to determine their gravitational interactions and movements in space. These theories were tested and confirmed to some degree in his 1899 Colorado Springs experiments. The U.S. government never gave Tesla the time of day, and his great electropropulsive discovery slipped into the eager hands of the Nazi elite, when Wernher von Braun acquired and began development of the "p2" project at Los Alamos, New Mexico in 1936, taking the project back to Germany in the fall of 1937, where it was developed at Peenemunde in the Baltic, until these secrets and others were traded to American corporations and the U.S. government in exchange, under *Operation Paperclip*, just after the armistice, for amnesty for many war criminals, along with an agreement for several thousand people to work for the U.S. government and American corporations. Anyone having important technical information was protected.

The REAL Cover-up

Ever since Tesla's saucer discovery came under the control of the U.S. government in 1945, there has been in effect a false propaganda program---originally developed by the *RSHA Amt VI (Reichsicherheithaupt Amt VI*---which translates to "National Security Agency Division 6"---the organization within the Gestapo which was invested with the highest secrets of the German Reich, and which controlled in Nazi Germany the equivalent to our own UFOlogy, new age, and pseudo-sceptic misinformation dissemination network). The government simply employed the whole Nazi saucer counterintelligence apparatus, and it was some of the original Nazi misinformationists, employed at Holloman A.F.B., New Mexico, who designed and implemented the 1947 "Roswell Hoax". Though shadowed with ostensible military and "national security" vestiges, this cover-up has been protracted on behalf of a coercive monopolist corporate state, even since the acquisition of the secrets by the Nazis in 1936, for if the technology had gotten even into the hands of private Germans at that time, the Nazi state's days would have been ever much more so shortly numbered.

Can you imagine the effect of this kind of transportation in private hands? It would allow the common man to go everywhere in the world, to visit all the places which he cannot presently even afford the airline fare to. Yet a small, privately-owned flying saucer would cost less than an automobile to build, would use practically no fuel, would travel thousands of miles per hour, would last a long time, and would require practically no maintenance.

Can you imagine the effect it would have on totalitarian communist, fascist, or corporate state governments and 'favored' economic interests? Can you see the bottom drop out of the candy-assed real estate market, when it suddenly became possible to live anywhere, even places where there were no roads? Can you see the problems along the borders of countries, when saucers fly across and back without checking through "customs"? The main problems, as you can see, are with the paranoid and criminal fears of power crazy authorities, who would suddenly lose a lot of the power necessary for them to keep their "jobs", protecting and maintaining the interests of the coercive elite.

These considerations are the ones which indicate the perpetrators of any "cover-up". There is much talk on TV programs, radio talk shows, newspapers, books, magazines, and videos about a "...cover-up of our government doing business with the aliens for fifty years". If you can see it on prime-time TV every night of the week, the only "cover-up" which can be presumed, is one which is opposite to the one they pretend to be telling you about. Such programs are the cover-up. The volume of these lies is so great that it is almost incredible, considering the fact that they are evidence of our own government covertly acting behind the scenes to lie to us. Whenever government is involved in broadcasting such trashy BIG LIES to every household in America, it is good cause to ask, "What else are they lying to us about?"

This book, along with my prior one, is dedicated to the objective of bringing this secret technological and socio-economic dictatorship to an end.

CHAPTER I: THE OCCULT ETHER THEORY AND ELECTROPULSION ?

The theory which I espouse in this book is based on what can be corroborated throughout the words and developments of Nikola Tesla and their logically construed implications, in combination with other special information linked to that, as presented here and in my prior book, *Space Aliens From the Pentagon*. This theory is close to Tesla's *Dynamic Theory of Gravity*, and I like to think that it even makes some corrections that Tesla himself made or would have made, had he lived long enough.

Like most theories, this theory is incomplete, may contain errors, and will require further development, tests, corrections, and revisions, either by myself of by others in the future. I have stated here my basic thinking on the subject up to this time, which has progressed somewhat since my prior book, using my own terminology involving "Omni Matter" (A.K.A., "the Ether"). If you will notice in my title to this chapter, I have already created another new word---"Electropulsion"--- to shorten the word "Electropropulsion".

Since this book is for the greatly uninformed public, as well as for the researcher, I will make an effort to couch it in layman's terms---for I am myself a layman---and will provide some illustrations where helpful, to give a reasonable grasp of my concepts, rather than a "quantum mechanical" mathematical orgy, which is usually combined with pages of dull equations and numbers which proceed logically from the contradictory and unproven illogical premises which are so prized by that ilk. It is as if to say, "Hey! Look at me Ma, I can do lots of math!"

"Ether Physics", by its very nature and name, is subatomic physics, which to me means "sub-protonic" and "sub-electronic". I am not so concerned with sub-atomic nuclear particles per se, but rather with what I believe are the finite building blocks of the proton and electron, which exist within the ether in simpler form. I will leave all the quarks, muons, mesons, leptons, etc., to the "Relativistic Quantum Mechanics" (hence, "R.Q.M.s"), and their "elegant equations".

Characteristics of Basic Ether Particles

My basic ether particle is called the "Omni", which has a positive nucleus---a "protette" called an "Omnion"---and a negative sub-electron---an "electrette" called an "Omnitron". As you may have noticed, this scheme is a scaled-down version of the basic hydrogen atom, with its proton and electron. Like most atoms, the Omni is normally neutral and in equilibrium, but is much smaller, being ultra-fine. Due to its tiny size and neutrality, it can pass easily through "solid bodies" (except the solid bodies are actually passing by and through it), yet it behaves like a solid in respect to high frequency electromagnetic radiation of specific range, from the infra-red through the visible light frequencies, which disturb its equilibrium, yet, though we can feel it, it appears to be transparent and invisible to the naked eye.

Like hydrogen gas, there is some elasticity, due to the compressibility of the magnetic fields, so it is an "elastic solid" as Faraday said. Due to the tiny Omni size, so-called "empty space" is actually packed almost solid with this very fine matter, which oscillates at such high frequencies---well beyond that of x-rays---yet the tiny size and normal neutrality allows it to penetrate "solid mass"---which is mostly "space"(which is also saturated with Omni which must be moved through by a mass to make room for more Omni).

Since interstellar 'space' is equivalent to a vacuum containing little gaseous matter---such as a Lenard tube in which charges easily move--- the Omni in interstellar space is highly conductive, with charges moving freely from body to body, along magnetic lines of force.

Omni-packed space is also omnidirectionally interpenetrated by ultra-fine radiation, which is normally in equilibrium, called "Zero Point Radiation" ("ZPR"). This ZPR constantly "twangs" the electron clouds of atomic matter, creating the illusion of "electron orbits", which are in fact standing waves in the undulating layers of electronic clouds surrounding atoms and molecules. Since the matter with which these electron clouds are associated is in constant motion, the clouds are currents, since a "charge carried around is a current". The driving force behind the currents is the motion, which, so long as uniform, is "force-free". Any lost momentum is 'made up' by the ZPR.

The Omni has an almost balanced charge-to-mass ratio ("1:1"), and responds to both positive and negative impulses. Electrostatic generators provide a good example of the electrical behavior of the Omni. At sufficiently high voltages, the positive and negative dynamic sub-charges are separated by magnetic fields and condensed to form electrons and protons. There is some unknown underlying reason why these charges are of specific magnitude, which is yet to be explained, but the quantum theory practically admits that there are subdivisions of basic electrical charges, and that electrons are not "indivisible". This the basic bone of contention, since if electrons *are* divisible, Relativism must fall. The "basic charge" which has been perceived as that of the electron, appears to be time-related, since electrical current moves at the same speed as light, therefore, the electron charge is probably the quantity of charge accumulated from a discrete number of Omni over some discrete unit of time, which reflects in turn the distance traveled through space of a proton during that time, with the charges actually circulating between the Omni and matter.

High voltage force—either in electrical discharges or in radiation—is necessary to break the Omnion-Omnitron bond. The same principle applies to electropulsion. Strong, high voltage, high frequency negative pulses are necessary to penetrate the negative Omnitronic cloud barriers, to react with the positive Omnions, to cause the "inertia resistance" of the Omni to be "asserted", so as to access its mass to be pulled against, to propel a space ship through Omni-packed space, using a microhelical "screwing" force of rotating electromagnetic tubules around irrotational, vacuous Omni cores. The tubules are the product of the rotation imparted by magnetic flux to electrical currents, which are consolidated by changes in momentum.

The great number of Omni per volume of space represents a much greater density of positive matter than normal 'solid' mass possesses, hence the Omni function as "virtually stationary anchors" which an electropulsive craft can lock onto to propel itself through space. The Omni 'anchors' are in fact dynamic relative to earth, with a relative velocity of thousands of miles per hour which represents the ultimate velocity of the earth through the ether at any given time. Since the "accessing" electropulsive force, when in effect, is transmitted at near the velocity of light however, the comparative difference in velocity between the Omni and the earth is almost insignificant. It is practically "as if" the earth is stationary relative to the ether, except for the effects of so-called gravity. To an effect which travels at 186,000 miles per second, a body traveling at about 20 miles per second is *virtually* "at rest".

The difference in density between liquid hydrogen and the Omni, for example, is relative to the difference in size between the hydrogen atom and the tiny Omni, as well as to the volume of space actually occupied by the Omnion in relation to its Omnitron. It can be assumed that a tiny Omnion, being a subdivision of the proton, has a much greater density per unit of space, due to the relative lack of space between the Omni, which assemble to form protons, much like the space between bricks which is filled with mortar. This 'mortar' is probably some of Tesla's "insulative fluid" which "wets" positive bodies and 'particles', as a "perfect fluid". Just as the magnitude of the electron charge may be time-relative, the magnitude of the proton may be likewise, being composed of a discrete number of Omnions accumulated over a discrete period of time.

    While the Omni is invisible to the eye---because its period of vibration is beyond the visible frequencies---it is not imperceptible. As we move, we can feel the Omni accelerating, decelerating, or changing directions within our bodies. When running, we feel the resistance ("inertia") created within our body, to changes in momentum, as the Omni tubules are forced in different directions or in accelerating or decelerating pathways through the atoms and molecules of our body. Once we reach a constant velocity, we can feel how the microhelices--- created by the constant-pitch spins of the Omnitrons---'bore' through the Omni, creating the "momentum" which tends to carry us along in level and straight lines. Once in constant velocity, we must supply only whatever energy is lost through wind or mechanical friction, or erratic movement, in order to maintain constant velocity. We can also see the effects of the Omni in the behavior of everyday objects---the way they resist changes in movement, fall, accelerate, gain momentum, tumble, roll, collide, shatter, bounce, or come to rest. I analogize a solid mass to a flock of geese, maintaining its "formation" ("shape"), as it flies through the "air" ("Omni"):

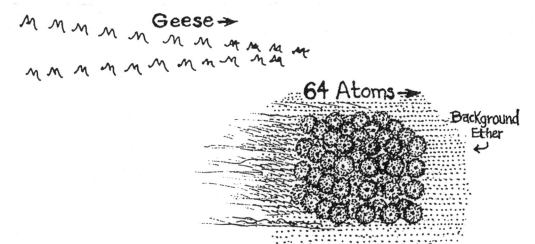

13

The earth and everything on it is moving through ether-filled space, at tremendous speed. In addition, the earth spins and orbits, which gradually changes the microhelical patterns relative to the polarity of an interpenetrating "etheric wind". The magnitude of the so-called "force of gravity", measured from the center of mass of a body, is greater at sea level than on top Mt. Everest, where the distance between its center and that of the earth is greater, but this statement---based on Newton's law---fails to tell us "why" gravity exists, what forces create it, or why the force varies "directly proportional to the masses, and inversely proportional to the square of the distance between (the centers of the) two bodies". Even Newton explicitly admitted that his laws failed to address causes, and only claimed to mathematically describe effects.

"Electrical content" is inherent to all solid matter. Atoms contain nuclei composed of positive protons and neutral neutrons, composed of protons and electrons. Around these nuclei are negative "electrons". All matter which contains electrostatic charges and is in motion, represent "electric charges carried around", hence currents, which create magnetic fields. Since magnetic fields impart rotation to electromagnetic fields, this creates rotatory microhelical electromagnetic tubules within bodies, around irrotational vacuous ether cores. These tubules are aligned by the relative motion of a body, along the axis of a uniform or changing movement, and create momentum by "boring through" the ether. Since at any given time the pitch and diameter of a microhelix is constant, it is not a "vortex", which involves a logarithmic spiral, either inward or outward. Each time the velocity or direction changes, the microhelical pitch and orientation resists, then adjusts to the new momentum.

The earth has a minimum negative surface charge of approximately 20 esu/cm^2 (20 electrostatic units per square centimeter). This is an atmospheric phenomenon due in part to the ionizing effects of cosmic radiation, but cannot be explained without reference to the velocity of the earth through the Omni. The relatively non-conductive, insulative and dielectric properties of the atmosphere play a part. Beneath the earth's surface charge, the semi-conductive crust contains a vast ocean of surplus electrons. The earth's surface charge is more or less a constant, due to earth's surface area, varying somewhat by altitude due to the changes in atmospheric pressure and moisture content of the air, as well as the incidence of cosmic radiation and its frequencies.

All atoms---including hydrogen---possess net positive charge. This is because the basic positive charge of a proton exceeds the magnitude of the basic negative charge of an electron. Hydrogen, with its single proton and single electron, has the highest charge-to-mass ratio and the lowest gravity of all elements. As one moves up the periodic chart of elements, progressively increasing in complexity above hydrogen, elements possess progressively lower charge-to-mass ratios, since the comparative ratios of electrons match the number of only the protons in the nuclei. Since the neutrons are not negative, they add to the positive mass relative to the electron, but contribute nothing to electrical charge, and the ratio of neutrons increases up the chart. This leaves an excess positive mass of the earth, the semi-conductive surface of which is capable of receiving and maintaining a large negative charge surplus, mostly brought to earth by the thousands of lightening bolts per second, and retained due to the dielectric and insulative properties of the atmosphere.

The constant electrical discharges from the atmosphere are driven by the cosmic motion of the earth, which converts the electrostatic charges to currents. This was confirmed by H.A. Rowland's experiment. Since atmospheric gases are insulators, the mostly alkaline, semi-conductive crust of the earth is largely an electron donor material, which maintains a large reservoir of negative charges insulated by the atmosphere. Cosmic rays striking the rarified light gases of the ionosphere, maintain its positive charge. The effects of gravity also help, since helium and hydrogen, both light, electropositive gases, gravitate to the ionosphere. Between the ionosphere, c. 620 miles above, and the earth's surface, there is a gradient of c. 150 volts/meter, totaling about 176 million volts, creating a considerable electric field, but the electric field extends far beyond the ionosphere. This electric field creates electrical displacement in the Omni within its reach, which is the cause of gravity. The effects of the electric field on the Omni is almost instantaneous, since near the speed of light, as the Omni pass from "free space" into mass, where the gravitational force is exerted downward, toward the source of the electric field.

There is no significant gravitational effect of earth's field above this electric field. Since earth's magnetic field encompasses the moon, so does the electric field. When a "sub-ion" (the Omni) is placed within an electric field, the sub-negative charge (Omnitron) is attracted by the positive pole (ionosphere) and repelled by the negative pole (earth). The effect of these attractive/repulsive forces is to "displace" each Omni, and to place the dielectric atmosphere and the Omni within a strain, so that, near the earth, the Omnitronic clouds around each Omnion are forced eccentrically upward, while the neutral zone would be over 300 miles from earth.

The Cause of the Apparent "Inverse Square" Law of Gravity

As earth spins, the surface velocity--- and atmospheric velocity with it---at any point varies according to its distance from earth's center. An object sitting at sea level moves through the Omni slower than a body on top Mt. Everest. The voltage potential between the atmospheric gases at higher altitude and the ionosphere is lower, but the voltage potential between the atmosphere and the surface of Mt. Everest is higher. Accordingly, for an object at sea level, the displacement of the Omnitronic cloud is greater, due to the greater total electric field strength. The increase in velocity offsets the increase in field effects on the Omni so that the gravitational force is more or less equalized between low and high altitude for objects on the earth, but the gravitational effects decrease for airborne objects beyond the earth's surface charges above Mt. Everest.

The differences in these electrical potentials illustrates why there are differences in relative displacement of the Omnitronic clouds, within both earth's "gravity field", and within bodies moving within that field, with a degree of displacement which is directly proportional to difference in so-called "gravitational force" and the dielectric strain.

This comparison shows that a body at a higher altitude and velocity has a lower gravity because the electric field has a lower displacing influence on the Omnitronic cloudlets, and vice-versa. This is pertinent to electropulsion, because we must diminish, reverse, magnify and otherwise control this displacement in order to instantly synthesize and control inertia, momentum, and "gravity". The displacement influences the momentum because it affects the vibrating microhelical tubules and the way they "bore" through etheric space. Since the electric field is somewhat blocked out inside solid bodies, the tubules tend to drop to concentric rotation, thus transferring a downward force to the mass of which they are a part. "Gravity" is a product of the resistance to this change in displacement. The reason why a moving sphere when charged experiences an increase in its "virtual mass"---that is, an increase in the work required to move it, but not in its gravity--- is because the "Faraday cage" effect of the increased charges tends to increase the resistance to the movement of the Omni through the mass, affecting the negative charges on the Omni.

Since the electric field and its displacing influence is altered by the difference in dielectric constant within and without solid bodies, the microhelical tubules tend to drop to concentric rotation, thus transferring a downward force to the mass of which they are a part. "Gravity" is a product of the resistance to this change in displacement.

Microhelical Tubes of Force

Due to the cosmic motion of earth, electrostatic, molecular charges become currents, which create magnetic fields within ponderable bodies. The currents and fields in atomic or molecular "domains" are unified by momentum or magnetic fields. As a body moves through the ether/Omni field with the earth, there is an "etheric wind" effect, which "blows through" mass constantly from a regularly changing direction. Since Omnitrons are "sub-electrons", they also resonate. As the electric content forms pathways through the Omni within the body, the resonant motions of the molecular currents form magnetic fields which impart the microhelical rotation of the plane of polarization around irrotational Omni cores. These microhelical "tubes" have "pitch" which is determined by the rate of linear movement per second, in conjunction with the diameters of their rotations (or "waves") at near the speed of light. These tiny waves have spherical fronts, which can combine to form larger spherical waves.

The microhelical tubes of electromagnetism, having pitch, function like drills, tending to bore straight paths at a constant pitch and linear velocity, around the irrotational vacuous Omni cores (consistent with Newton's laws for inertia and momentum). Any change in direction or velocity is met by a resistance ("inertia"). Since all mass is already in motion, it always has momentum. The inertia exhibited by a body at rest relative to earth, is really a product of its momentum, so this inertia is really momentum. Inertia is therefore a resistance of a body to change in its state of momentum. The two words are used in different ways, to define "relative changes" in velocity and/or orientation.

Since the Omni near the spinning earth are subjected to the stronger negative charges and the positive mass of the earth, the Omnions are attracted downward, while the Omnitrons around them are repelled upward, forming eccentric 'cloudlets'. For a body ("at rest") at sea level, as the Omni enter its surface, the effects on the Omni of the electric field of the earth is altered by the change in dielectric constant, forcing the microhelical tubes in the mass to jump downward to a more concentric rotation, since the density and rigidity of the Omni resists such a change. Since the electromagnetic tubes are part of the mass, a downward force is created by the downward pressure of the Omitrons, which we call "gravity". The effect is similar to a water hose carrying a high pressure stream of water. The helical force of the water creates a gyroscopic stability and tends to straighten it out into a line, with a regular precession. The "straightening" action is analogical to the so-called "gravity force". This is true no matter which direction the solid body is moving through the ether, because of the relative speed of the electromagnetic interaction at virtually the speed of light, and the polarity of earth's electric field.

Gravity, therefore, is the product of a body's reaction to the Omni's resistance to a change in its momentum, transferred to a mass due to its difference in dielectric constant, and its constantly changing movement, orientation and velocity as it moves through universal etheric space.

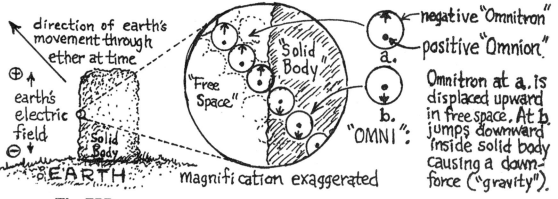

The ZPR

In addition to the Omni Matter, all space is omnidirectionally interpenetrated by ubiquitous Zero Point Radiation ("ZPR"), of extremely high frequencies, power, and density. One scientist has attributed so-called "blackbody radiation" to the ZPR (T.H. Boyer, *Derivation of Blackbody Radiation Spectrum Without Quantum Assumptions*, Phys. Rev. 182 [5], pp. 1374-83 [1969]). Boyer also found that a nonlinear dipole can absorb energy from particular modes of the ZPR spectrum (*Random Electrodynamics: The theory of classical electrodynamics with classical electromagnetic zero-point radiation*, <u>Phys. Rev.</u> D 11 [4], pp. 790-808 [1975]). Another scientist claimed to measure the energy density of ZPR at 10^{94} gram/cm^3, for individual fluctuations of random ZPR, on the scale of the Planck length (10^{-33} cm.), by means of a standard radiation detector, the frequency response of which was specially altered to extend into the super high frequency spectrum involved (J.A. Wheeler, *Geometrodynamics*, <u>Academic Press</u>, N.Y. [1962]). In my last chapter, I detail the extraction of ZPR energy in the atomic hydrogen process.

These particular researches of 1962 to 1975 are *ex post facto*, coming long after Tesla's great discoveries. They merely re-confirm that, in order for such intense, super high frequency radiation to pass through space, it would require a space literally packed with an even finer ether, consisting of dense, super high frequency, ultrafine bundles of positive mass, surrounded by sub-electronic negative charges. This combination, like the continously interlinked tetrahedronal silicon dioxide atoms which make up solid quartz crystals, is capable of reacting to and conducting electromagnetic radiation from the infinitely fine in frequency, to the coarsest frequencies, simultaneously in all directions ("omnidirectionally"). This dense matter behaves as a solid to lower frequency radiation between the x-ray spectrum down to the lower infra-red, yet behaves as an all-pervading, interpenetrating and all-wetting "perfect fluid", in respect to (the atomic content of) moving solid bodies, the atomic structures of which contain so much room that they are mostly "space".

Electropulsion utilizes externally projected IR-to visible frequency radiation, of very high voltage, to cause the Omni to assert its "inertia resistance", combined with low frequency internal waves to create the (polarized) rotatory electromagnetic tubules, which instantaneously synthesize momentum, by boring through the ether-filled space, to propel a spacecraft through it.

An Old Wooden Box and a German Inertial Guidance System

In 1979, at a Santa Fe flea market, I examined an old wooden box belonging to an elderly Pojoaque man who was employed as a workman in 1937 at a secret project called "p2", which was run by Wernher von Braun. The man had built the box to hold tools used in his job there. He had carved, in "New Mexico folk style", a "map" showing the highways, the location and name of the project, the symbol for the project (a triangle with a dot in its center, which is a symbol for the Prussian Illuminati of which von Braun was a member), and the date of the project. Pojoaque---where the man lived---is prominently shown as a large "P" with a zia sign around it. Below is my drawing of the old box:

The following weekend, in the spring of 1979, I went to an Albuquerque salvage company---"King's Surplus City"---on east Central, where I often bought military surplus things related to my research and inventing, and was pleased to find a very unusual pile of material all stacked in a separate little pile. On top the pile was a device which I immediately recognized as a type of navigational "compass" which would be required on the early flying saucers I had witnessed during my back yard sleepouts in Kermit, Texas, between 1949-53, which turned in increments of multiples of thirty degrees. The device showed thirty-degree increments, and had 14 contacts---twelve for each of the directions, and two for the six-volt motor which rotated the compass ring---and the label showed it was manufactured in Nazi Germany by Lizt on Oct. 1, 1943, in lot 127-178 (52 devices), for a project named "KT-p2" ("Kreisel Teller - p2", which meant "Gyrating Saucer - p2"). The device was called a "Peiltochterkompass" (a "polar slave compass"), which was controlled by signals from a "Meisterkreiselkompass" (a "master gyro-compass"), which means that the device was half of an inertial guidance system.

Photos of the device are shown below:

```
Peiltochterkompass
      KT-p2
Gerat Nr.    127-178 A-1
Anforderz.   FI 23374
Werk Nr.     10143
Hersteller:  g v y
```

The letters "p2", which designated the 1937 Los Alamos project run by von Braun, were incorporated into the official secret name-designation for the Nazi flying saucer project in 1943 Germany.

As explicitly detailed in *Space Aliens*, I saw the original reels of gun camera films made during WWII over northern Germany, in 1957, later in the afternoon of the same day that Major Donald Kehoe carried out his hoax on national TV. Some of the films had been made by some of the same men then present, since my Air Force Intelligence group was attached to the original U.S. Army Eighth Air Force group which had conducted those particular bombings in B-17 bombers. Those films showed what were apparently manned "flying turtles"---small electropulsive craft---which flew at high speeds around the bombers, in order to draw fire and interfere with their missions.

In the spring of 1945, as the Russians closed in on Berlin, General

George Patton took a special armored group deep into Russian-encircled territory, to the Nazi rocket center at Peenemunde on the Baltic. Attached to this group, disguised as "tank commanders", were Army intelligence officers specially vested with the task of retrieving all flying saucer materials and/or destroying the same at the Peenemunde project, along with retrieval of any technical drawings, etc. of strategic importance at the project, before it could be captured by the Russians. On discovering 200 celestial guidance systems (A.K.A., "inertial" guidance systems) deep underground in a salt cave, General Patton was infuriated on being ordered to destroy these systems by his superiors, being unaware of the fact that the technical drawings and specifications for the systems were already in American possession.

Development of the systems was imperative for the flying saucer, since a magnetic compass would be worthless due to the "Faraday cage" effect of the electric field surrounding the saucer, which would block out the magnetic field of the earth. The master gyro was calibrated to true north prior to takeoff, and would continue to hold that position during flight, so that the "slave" compass would have that as a reference, in order to actuate the six-volt motor and turn the geared compass heading ring to reflect the correct direction of flight. This particular type of Peiltochterkompass was used on a circular ship which could turn peripherally—in 360 degrees, frontwards, sideways, backwards, etc., in increments or multiples of 30 degrees---while other devices were used on some of the latest types of German "V" ("Vergetungswaffen", or "Revenge-weapons") rockets, which carried neutron bomb warheads, and were fired from underwater from special small submarines which were towed behind the latest "Electro-U-Boats" used in the final "Stalemate" which I detailed in *Space Aliens*.

Subsequent to my purchase, security agents learned of my possession of it and knowledge of what it was, so they went to Mark King, son of the owner of King's Surplus City, and grilled him. He showed them the bill of sale from Sandia Base, pursuant to his purchase of the small pile of salvage from a Sandia Base employee who usually brought salvage from that base to sell to him. As it turned out, the man had stolen a pile of classified salvage and sold it for his own profit, using a 'double-receipt' process intended to cover his tracks, but the security people put the man under surveillance, caught him doing it again, and charged, convicted and jailed him. They could not get the device back from me, because I was an "innocent purchaser", and because it would confirm the still-classified purpose of the device, in violation of security procedures. I had purchased an inertial guidance system from a 1943 Nazi flying saucer, which has subsequently been brought to Sandia Base in late 1945 under Operation Paperclip, along with what was later to be over 116 flying saucer scientists and over 15,000 German personnel who were brought to New Mexico, as part of a special secret "deal" which was cut pursuant to the Stalemate.

As to the question of what "p2" meant scientifically, a similar designation was used by Nikola Tesla to denote "potentials", "plates", or "primaries". The drawing which follows is derived from information contained in Tesla's 1890's lectures and excerpted on pages 70-73, and provides the best clues I have found as to how Tesla created his "p2":

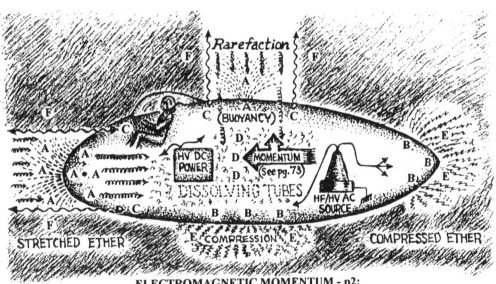

ELECTROMAGNETIC MOMENTUM - p2:

A - D.C. Potential - Carriers exchange in Brush (negative corona) - Tubes of Force enter conductors which are attached firmly to ship's structure
B - A.C. Potential - Carriers compressed - Tubes of Force exit blocked
C - Tesla Bulbs polarize Tubes of Force - space rendered conductive
D - Trapped Tubes of Force Dissolved - Momentum imparted at 10^{40} x fg
E - Compressed Carriers - Blocked Tubes - (positive A.C. corona)
F - Random Tubes of Force in free space

Both the D.C. 'brush' electrode and the A.C. 'compression' electrode would draw the ether carriers through the mass of the ship and its contents, creating the microhelical tubes which bored away around the ether. The electrode on the left would be assisted by the special Tesla bulbs, so that, when paired with the opposite A.C. electrode, it would increase the pitch angle of the microhelices, accelerating the ether through the mass and propelling the ship.

Low and High Frequency Electromagnetic Waves
And Tesla's Wireless Transmission of Energy

Low frequency electromagnetic waves can pass through solid bodies, and tend to "hug the earth", while high frequency waves don't penetrate solid bodies, causing a "skin effect" on them, and don't "hug the earth", but tend rather to travel outward away from the earth in straight lines. Nikola Tesla, in his *Colorado Springs Experiments*, was the first person to investigate high voltage waves of high and low frequency, and their terrestrial, atmospheric, and solid-body effects. The scope of Tesla's Colorado Springs experiments were so far-reaching, that very little or nothing was said in science journals about them, because they left other scientists so dumbfounded that they were paralyzed by miscomprehension.

Many of Tesla's tests in Colorado were related to electropulsion. A long wave affects the internal mass of a space ship, "synthesizing momentum", by invoking the rotatory motion of electromagnetism, to create the drill-like electromagnetic microhelices ("tubes of force") which "bore through" the ether as the mass moves. At the same time, a higher frequency at the opposite end of the ship, opposite to the direction of travel, causes the ether to be accelerated as it passes through the mass of the ship and its contents, with an increased angle of pitch, so the microhelical boring action propels the ship through space.

Low frequency waves also make it possible to project forceful longitudinal electromagnetic pulses to a specific, distant point, by sending the wave along a conductor or polarized atmospheric "carrier beam" of U.V. or higher frequency radiation. The high voltage long wave, carried directionally to a distant point by the carrier beam, can in turn carry additional higher frequency waves superimposed on it, to deliver the high frequency exciting energy, at the powerful long-wave peaks. This was the basis for Tesla's "Transmission of Electrical Energy Without Wires" inventions, as well as his "energy beam" and "death ray" inventions, as the same system can be used for all three. The manipulation of these wave characteristics is inextricably involved in electropulsion, stimulated by Tesla's study of the works of 19th century "ether physicists", and his own brilliant creative intuitions of the rotating magnetic field, in Budapest Hungary, in 1882. This rotating magnetic field discovery was involved in his electropulsion discovery, because Tesla realized that the rotatory force of magnetic fields could be used to synthesize the rotating "tubes of force", the naturally occurring phenomena in solid bodies spoken of by Faraday and Maxwell and known to Tesla, to propel a ship through space. The tubes had also been discussed in 1881, by J.J. Thomson in England, but Thomson had never related the tubes specifically to the ether until after Nikola Tesla had connected the tubes to his intended electropulsion.

Tesla discovered that by using a low frequency beam-directed pulse, he could cause, at the quarter wavelength, the eruption of a large electromagnetic pulse which could, by carrying a much higher exciting wave, excite the atmospheric gases in a region, to explosively expand them, followed by a tremendous implosion and the absorption of a great amount of heat in the area, causing immediate freezing. This process would create an initial explosive shock wave followed by the implosive return wave, similar to nuclear detonation. For example, by using a low frequency of 60 cps, with a wavelength of 3,100 miles, directed by carrier-beam, a pulse could be made to erupt at one-quarter wavelength---775 miles, corrected to 751 miles by velocity factor. By superimposing an exciting frequency of say 50 megahertz or so, the atmospheric gases could be excited to cause a "cold implosion" which absorbs heat. By altering the wavelength and the direction of propagation, the results could be delivered to any terrestrial point.

The Tesla ion bulb, fundamental to Tesla's "beams", is a solid aluminum hemisphere, enclosed in a glass vacuum envelope, excited by high voltage D.C. applied to the center of the hemispherical end. A polarized beam is emitted normal to the flat face center. The frequency is determined by the voltage. The ion beam polarizes, concentrates, and guides a spherical, long wave front, amplified by Tesla's "extra coil", to a distant target, which amplifies a higher frequency wave front superimposed upon it, which will "ring" in the target area at one-quarter wavelength, in fact ring many times.

Outside the bulb, in close proximity to the beam, the high voltage alternating current ("power wave") of low frequency, is emitted by a ring-shaped electrode, and is directed along the beam's atmospherically created conductive path, and is projected toward the distant target where the one-quarter wave peak delivers it at its "point" of greatest potential. This idea of Tesla's may have been stimulated by Maxwell's

25

concept that conductivity actually occurs in the dielectrics surrounding a conductor, with the 'conductor' serving only to "guide" the current.

The June 30, 1908 Siberian explosion/implosion at Tungushka, was probably a risky test or inadvertent result of Tesla's giant Wardenclyffe oscillator, and may have been a hidden reason as to why the project was never completed. It should also be pointed out that this method involved the absorption of energy "from the environment", since heat moves from hot to cold. This was yet another great energy discovery. Tesla's method "opened up" the atmosphere to this possibility, consistent with what he said about nuclear energy coming from "the environment".

The Tungushka explosion may also have been the impetus for a "very tempting offer" made to Tesla years before by V.I. Lenin, mentioned in retrospect in a November 29, 1934 letter from Tesla to J.P. Morgan (microfilm, Library of Congress). The Lenin offer would have been between 1917 and 1934, and was mentioned unsuccessfully in attempt to tantalize Morgan). Tesla's "particle beam" weapon was hinted at in the following illustration:

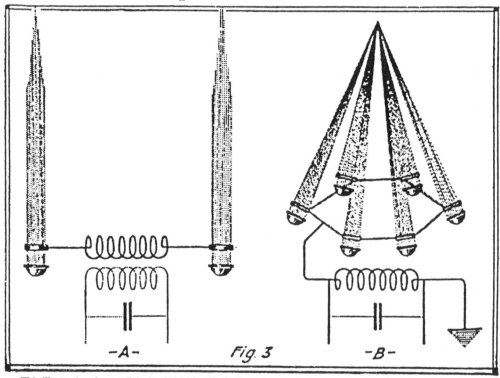

This illustration, from a July 11, 1934 *New York Times* article, shows several of the special solid aluminum Tesla bulbs which, as Tesla stated in 1940 (see page 27), no longer required vacuum. The current is placed on the beams by means of the ring-shaped electrodes near each bulb, fed with currents from the coils.

Tesla's TELEFORCE Discoveries

Tesla's Teleforce discoveries, evolved between 1900 and 1940, consisted of a "new" way to produce rays in free air without a vacuum, a "new" way to create a "very great electrical force", a "new" way of "magnifying" the force, and a "new" means of electro-propulsion (William L. Laurence, *New York Times*, Sept. 22, 1940, 11, p. 7). These four "new" discoveries---all of which could work together---were actually a juxtaposition of and different application of Tesla's devices already tested separately in the Colorado Springs experiments or later in New York or Wardenclyffe, with the exception that by 1915, he had tested the electropulsive missile powered by beam-projected electrical energy, and had tested a small, one-man electropulsive prototype in which he ventured out his hotel window at night over New York City in experimental test flights, and which served as an experimental basis for a much larger and more ambitious set of space ships which he had designed, which were repeatedly rejected by the U.S. government, probably because they thought he was nuts.

Even the Nazis were skeptical that the Tesla electro-propulsive technology might work, being unconvinced until Wernher von Braun had actually tested the concepts at Los Alamos in 1936 and 1937, and obtained the final approval of Hitler. Almost immediately after von Braun's return to Germany in late 1937, construction was begun on large "cigar-shaped" ships, using at first the iron pressure hulls of U-boats, which were already equipped with a hermetically sealable system carrying diesel generators for use in the atmosphere, and batteries for use in outer space. With the huge difference between the strength of the electromagnetic interaction and gravity, weight was apparently no object.

Since Tesla had actually received offers from the Russians prior to that time, I had considered the possibility that he had knowingly or unknowingly cooperated somehow with the Nazis in their Los Alamos experiments, through some of the unidentified laboratories he said he was working with, which is a very real possibility.

In looking for a probable Nazi spy, there was one who had wormed his way into Tesla's most intimate confidences, who was later convicted and imprisoned for his espionage activities in America, but the exact nature of his activities, other than the dissemination of Nazi propaganda, was never specified in the public records. This connection was the most probable explanation for how Tesla's electropulsive discoveries found their way to the Nazi "p2" project, with all elements coinciding perfectly in time. The fact that von Braun's pre-war New Mexico adventures have been subsequently concealed from the public by the Secret Government, a degree of secrecy which cannot be explained except by reference to the Nazi flying saucer projects, is compelling.

The fact that I was a personal friend to an American rocket scientist named Peter van Dresser, who was angered by Dr. Robert Goddard's pre-war work with von Braun, and who was present in New Mexico since the '20's and was intimately familiar with the 1930's liaisons to von Braun's secret Los Alamos activities, left little remaining to be proven, since there is no longer any security basis for concealing such liaisons, if "rocket research" was the only thing von Braun's pre-war American presence involved. He had already been appointed as the Peenemunde project research leader, and had been promoted by Hitler and Himmler to *Ubersturmbannfuehrer* in the SS, and was given a "leave of absence" by Hitler to make the venture to America.

Dr. Robert Goddard, whose New Mexico laboratory was at Mescalero, with his launch area at Eden Valley, near Roswell, far to the south, was not involved in any known pre-WWII research at Los Alamos, and probably knew nothing of von Braun's secret project there.

One of the most telling pieces of evidence regarding the intentional misinterpretation of Tesla's discoveries---especially just after Tesla's death in Jan., 1943, at which point all Tesla's papers and apparati fell into the hands of the FBI---is the obvious meaning of the name for his system---"TELEFORCE"---which means "force at a distance", in the context of the four listed parts of the system to be used together, being clearly applicable to <u>flying saucer propulsion</u>, once I pointed out the fraud, and correctly interpreted the statement in 1993.

I have to hand it to the spooks, for doing such a good job of concealing the connection between the flying saucer and the only man who could have invented it---and whom the public should most readily accept as the inventor who rightfully deserved the credit for it---even though he never had a fair opportunity of giving his greatest discovery to the world, for lack of money to build a working model of sufficiently developed potential to impress us. The reason why he never had the money was because of the secret "bill of attainder" placed on his name by the greedy monopolists who were and still are afraid of technological freedom and a truly free market of ideas, goods, and services.

CHAPTER II: EXPLORING THE NATURE OF THE ETHER

The Early Background

In 1997, after many years of research and thought regarding the qualities of the ether, I decided to see what others had actually said, before completing this book. Some of the material available to me was second-hand information, being what someone said someone else had said. I wanted to make sure these "repeated statements" were accurate. After some difficulty, I accessed a copy of the classic, *A History of the Theories of the Aether and Electricity*, by Sir Edmund Whittaker (1951 revised and enlarged second edition, Vols. I and II). The 1910 first edition of this book was probably the most comprehensive book ever published on ether theory as it existed in 1910, but the 1951 revision merely clarified "acceptable" ether physics. The first edition was printed in Scotland, under the title *A History of the Theories of the Ether and Electricity, from the age of Descartes to the close of the nineteenth century*. The second edition incorporated "new material" related to quantum mechanics. Classical theory was in Vol. I, while Vols. II and III gave the origins of relativity and quantum theory up to 1926. Neither the 1910 first edition nor the 1951 revision mentioned Tesla, but the chronological sequence appeared to be "skewered"in the revised edition, with little or no attempt to point out what the scientists were actually aiming at in terms of electropulsion. Though information regarding Nikola Tesla was omitted, there is much valuable related information.

In his preface, Whittaker stated that where space is now considered "emptiness"---except for its property of propagating electromagnetic waves---the development of quantum electrodynamics referred to a vacuum with a new status as the location of 'zero point' oscillations of the electromagnetic fields and zero point fluctuations of electric charge and current, as well as a polarization conforming to that of a dielectric constant, which is non-unity (i.e., which contains energy). This implies awareness of the ZPR, but quantum theory inherently excludes the possibility of "zero-point" fluctuations, since all such waves are always regarded as possessing one-half "quantum".

Whittaker said that an alleged failure by ether theory proponents to observe the earth's motion relative to the ether, caused the downfall of the theory, but the facts show that the relativists, backed by corporate publishing interests, hastily dug the grave and threw the dirt over the

29

corpse of ether theory while it was still alive, for the wrong reasons. Much of the error was due to focusing on the weakest proponents who believed that a portion of the ether is "carried along" by the earth, and that an optical aberration would have to be observed at some point away from the earth, in order for an ether to exist. It was asserted that the failure of this observation was the "death" of "the" ether theory. By advertising ether theory's weakest and most erroneous proponents and ideas, the media made the RQM's hasty funeral of ether theory easy, and paved the way for the gullible public's acceptance of relativism.

I concluded that Whittaker's 1951 edition intentionally skewered important facts concerning electropulsion, which I have attempted to straighten out for you in this book. I now feel more comfortable with my version of Tesla's theory, than I did prior to reading Whittaker's book, but that was only because I knew what I was looking for. The facts I found are almost exactly as I said in my second edition of *Space Aliens*.

By reorganizing Whittaker's material into more proper order, I discovered much "new" ("old") documentation, that 19th century scientists were in pursuit of electropropulsion, and that there were interesting similarities between the thinking of certain scientists of the era and my own, which could eliminate some erroneous concepts about what they actually said, and shows similarities to what I observed on numerous occasions in the behavior of electropulsive "flying saucers", since the "proof of the pudding" is when it flies across the dinner table. It was my intent to examine known theory leading up to Tesla, to see what he contributed to their discoveries, and to determine what happened since that time to obscure, misinterpret and ultimately conceal it. To this end, I present for you a brief history and documentation of pertinent ether physics.

J.J. Thomson's "Electromagnetic Momentum"

Returning to the concept of the "carry-along" ether, Max Planck, originator of quantum mechanics, conscribed to this form of ether theory in part, saying that the ether had to be irrotational, carried along at the same velocity as earth near its surface, and compressible and subject to gravity like the atmosphere, in order for the theory to be true. At best, Planck's belief's showed a weak mechanical conceptualization, something unexpected from one purportedly so adept at "mechanics".

J.J. Thomson (1856-1942), discoverer of the electron, conscribed to

30

a different and more plausible ether theory. Thomson had theorized---based on Maxwell's earlier theory---that a charged spherical conductor moving in a straight line must produce displacement currents in the medium (<u>Phil. Mag</u>. xi [1881], p. 229). In 1893, twelve years later, he claimed to have discovered "electromagnetic momentum", saying "...in an electromagnetic field there is stored in every unit volume an amount of mechanical momentum, proportional to the vector product of the electric and magnetic vectors". (J.J. Thomson, <u>Recent Researches in Elect. And Mag.</u> [1893], p. 13.) Thomson also was said to have developed the theory of moving tubes of force---which harked back to Faraday's earlier work---saying in 1891 that molecular structure is closely connected with tubes of electrostatic force, with magnetism regarded as a secondary force. He stated that "...the aether itself is the vehicle of mechanical momentum, of amount $(1/4\pi C)$ [D·B] per unit volume." (<u>Phil. Mag</u>. xxxi [1891], p. 149; <u>Recent Researches in Elect. and Mag.</u> [1893], chap. 1.)

<u>Tesla Shows Up</u>

It is interesting to note that these "discoveries" by Thomson however, although following his initial speculations based on Maxwell's theory, also followed Tesla's lecture before the American Institute of Electrical Engineers at Columbia College, N.Y., on May 20, 1891, in which he described experiments in which he had earlier pre-empted Thomson's work with experimental verification, together with a demonstration of techniques and machinery built by him which obtained frequencies and voltages which W. Thomson (Lord Kelvin) had said earlier in England, were "impossible to achieve". In that sense, the "good old boys" in Britain should have admitted that Tesla's work was prior, after having acquiesced in the admission without rebuttal, that "they" were unable to create the equipment to produce the required frequencies to investigate and to experimentally verify these phenomena.

J.J. Thomson's theory, which linked electromagnetism with momentum in a mathematical and unified way, <u>on paper</u>, somewhat repeated Tesla's earlier lecture of 1891, proven by his earlier experiments, but Tesla's theory was different from Thomson's, whose theory was incorrect. Thomson's electromagnetic momentum could be created instantaneously only with Tesla's contrivances, which existed before Thomson's "discovery", only in Tesla's laboratory, so there is no way that Thomson could have reduced "his" theory to practice or experimentally verified it.

Though the facts show that Thomson was prior to Tesla in *attempting* to publish a valid theory, Tesla could not publish prior to perfection of his invention, which was not a factor affecting Thomson. Tesla was first to prove his theory by experimental results. Tesla remained more than a gentleman about it, deferring often to Thomson, though Thomson even attempted later to dishonestly claim Tesla's alternating current and high frequency discoveries. Thomson's earlier work (<u>Phil. Mag.</u> xi [1881], p. 229), concerning a charged spherical conductor, moving in a straight line, had commanded Tesla's respect and probably influenced his work, but Tesla's 1884 discovery of the rotating magnetic field had already beaten them all to the punch, and documentation shows that he had arguments with his "learned professors" in Graz, who said he must be "crazy", from his 1870's student days, to prove it.

It must have worked a horrible hardship on Tesla, to remain silent about his complete theory, which he could not publish without giving away his technology, before he could perfect a working model to get patent protection. It was like the Wardenclyffe tower, turning in the wind of incompleteness for lack of money, created by having been falsely induced into building an expensive system which would exhaust his energy and financial resources to the point of bankruptcy.

In respect to momentum, I would analogize it as follows: When a body is held by a spinning or arcing arm, it contains the changing tubes of force created by angular momentum. When released, it moves in a straight line vector, corresponding to the state of the tubes of force at the time of release. While held by the arm, centrifugal force was created by the tendency of the tubes to move in a straight line, or at least to continue whatever transverse or complex pattern of movement of the tubes which then existed, which created the resistance to change by the tubes at any moment. Once released, "something" (the microhelical tubes of force, as they then existed) determined its direction of movement and velocity, which in a vacuum would be force-free. These facts are consistent with Tesla's (Thomson's, Faraday's, Maxwell's) "tubes of force", which I will explain later in greater detail.

Most of Thomson's 1881 work harked back to Maxwell, and before him, Faraday, who had stated in 1831 that movement of an electrostatically charged body is equivalent to a current, which was described as a tube of force created by movement and momentum (Faraday, <u>Experimental Res.</u> Sec. 1644; Maxwell, <u>Treatise</u>, Secs. 768-70).

In his consideration of the nature of "ponderable matter", Faraday had suggested that an atom may be nothing more than a field of force---electric, magnetic and gravitational---surrounding a point-centre, which is completely penetrable (Bence Jones' <u>Life of Faraday</u>, ii, p. 178). Fresnel later stated, 'Upon considering the aberration of the stars, I am disposed to believe that the luminiferous aether pervades the substance of all material bodies with little or no resistance, as freely perhaps as the wind passes through a grove of trees'. Fresnel's concept presupposed that the ether surrounding the earth was unaffected by earth's motion, and generally agrees with what is actually observed, except for his failure to consider how the earth's dynamic electric field affects the ether.

Along with his c.1831 theory of an (elastic) solid electric ether, and lines of magnetic force, Faraday considered all space as "filled".

Wm. Thomson (A.K.A. Lord Kelvin) (1824-1907), at age 17, based on Faraday's earlier announcements, introduced into mathematical science the idea of electric action at a distance by means of a continuous ether. In 1846, he analogized electric phenomena with mechanical elasticity. It was his early concept that material atoms move through the ether 'without displacing it or compressing it' (*letter*, <u>FitzGerald to Heaviside</u>, 4 Feb. 1889), concepts later to be adopted by Tesla in saying that the ether 'behaves as a fluid to solid bodies, and as a solid to light and heat'.

About 1853, Bernhard Riemann (1826-66) conceived an ether which resisted compression and changes of orientation (<u>Ann. D. Phys.</u> cxii [1867], p. 237; Riemann's <u>Werke</u>, 2e Aufl., p. 288; <u>Phil. Mag.</u> xxxiv [1867], p. 368).

Riemann thought the resistance to compression caused gravitational and electrostatic effects, while the resistance to changes in orientation caused optical and magnetic phenomena, but he failed to develop these concepts further. These early Riemann insights were however very influential on later thinkers. He conceived a stationary ether based on the generally accepted assumption that, as the earth moved through space, the ability of one to see a star with a steady image disproved a dynamic ether. As to the propagation of electric action through space, Riemann proposed a new equation in which voltage changes outward from charges with a velocity $\underline{C}$, but he also failed to follow up with a proper consideration of the properties of the ether, because he died too damned young. Riemann's insights were verified almost 50 years later, ten years longer than his entire lifetime.

Years later, Maxwell, after reading Faraday's 1831 <u>Experimental Researches in Electricity</u> (3 Vols.), formed a mechanical conception of the electromagnetic field, connecting Faraday's magnetic lines of force and electrical ideas with the mathematical analogies of Wm. Thomson, carrying Faraday's concepts a step further (I have always liked to say that Maxwell "put the math to Faraday", because Faraday couldn't do much math, though he is recognized as the greatest "experimental philosopher" in history, a former Irish bookbinder's journeyman who got his early education from the books he was binding, and who at age 21 happened to write a letter to chemistry professor Sir Humphrey Davy in 1812 and so impressed him that the following spring he was appointed a chair at the Royal Institution, and the rest is history). A sort of electrician's Mozart, Faraday like none other, was almost always right from the beginning, in the middle, and long after his death, with so many remarkable insights and observations which were made without resort to tiresome pages of math, lucky for Maxwell, who made his own contributions in the process.

Faraday had stated that induced magnetism in iron exists only within the iron, was zero in external free ether, and was the basis for electrical induction. Maxwell's "electric displacement in a dielectric" was analogous to the magnetic induction B, which he said may have a value different from zero <u>even in the free ether</u>. According to Maxwell, there is a displacement (i.e., an electric movement away from equilibrium position) wherever there is electric force, whether "material bodies" are present or not (thus carrying his electric displacement into the ether) (Maxwell, <u>Scientific Papers</u> i, p. 451; p. 526).

It had occurred to me that since the earth and bodies "at rest" on it are in uniform motion (or uniformly *changing* motion) in respect to a stationary ether, that there were differences in electric displacement of ether in the space within solid bodies and space within the free ether, due to the polarization of the ether by the electric field of the earth, and the differences in dielectric constant between the two. I deduced from this that the constant movement of bodies through a stationary ether-filled space, carrying their charges with them, creates the displacement currents.

Maxwell had represented Faraday's lines of magnetic force (vectors of magnetic induction) as the velocity of an incompressible fluid, based on Faraday's suggestion years earlier that there may be a "dynamical condition" similar to electric current, and that the 'physical lines of magnetic force are currents' of this "fluid". This agrees with Faraday's "dynamical condition" of the electric field 'carried along' by the earth, equivalent to a current, producing the earth's magnetic field and gravitation, by effects on the stationary ether within earth's dynamic electric field. It also implies that magnetic lines of force are the "equal and opposite" reaction to electrical current as Faraday stated, and *vice-versa*, though magnetic fields are more the secondary effect of electric currents. The magnetic field is equally important however, in its creation of the rotatory motion imparted to electricity, which is responsible for the microhelical "tubes of force" which create the momentum which maintains the perpetual motion of celestial bodies in the universe, and guides electric currents through the ether forever. And this sounds very much like it must have been Tesla's theory as well.

Cosmic Motion and Local Momentum

The earth orbits the sun at approximately 18.5 miles per second (66,600 mph). The solar system is orbiting the center of the Milky Way much faster, and the Milky Way orbits the Magellanic Clouds much faster, and so fourth. This hierarchy of velocity increases from the moon, to the earth, the Milky Way, etc., although these pale into insignifance relative to electromagnetic velocity, since movement of force is time-relative. In all, the earth's velocity and polarity relative to the ether continually varies according to its rotation, orbital position, and galactic cycle. When between the sun and the Milky Way's center, for example, it moves slower than when to the "outside". As the earth rotates each day, its polarity of movement through the ether rotates 15.2 degrees per hour, with a rotational surface velocity at the equator of approximately 1,041 mph. This continuous change in polarity is so gradual that it is sensually imperceptible, but probably contributes to modulating the gravity force (and may even influence our emotional states!).

According to W.B. Morton (<u>Phil. Mag.</u> xli [1896], p. 488), an increase in charge of a body increases its "virtual mass", which increases the work required to move it by amount $2e^2/3ac^2$. This was in correction of J.J. Thomson's figure. Such a case suggests a dynamo consisting of large, insulated conductive balls on the end of a shaft, which are alternately charged and discharged to alternately increase and decrease their masses, thus rotating the shaft. But this possibility appears to be a fantasy, since the "increase in work required to move the ball" (in Thomson's theory) is related to an increase in the resistance to the penetration by the ether, caused by the presence of the extra charges, which according to Faraday created a "Faraday cage" effect which shuts out the magnetic lines of force. Without the magnetic lines of force---or with suppressed or diminished lines of force---the rotation of the tubes of force by the magnetic field are diminished or stopped, resulting in a diminution or elimination of momentum. Such propositions give ample food for thought.

If Tesla had continued to increase the earth's charge with his gadgetry, he could have thrown the earth's timing off, slowed it down, and possibly caused it to drift toward the sun. Being aware of these facts, he later addressed them and even listed them as future technical possibilities, which also corroborated his developments in the field of electropulsion, in case anybody noticed.

Local Momentum and Celestial Movement

It's an odd thing, momentum. If a body is in motion relative to earth, its momentum is in the direction of motion, yet as a body at rest on a spot on earth, it still had momentum along the spot's ultimate motion relative to the ether. The motion is compound, but the ultimate momentum of a body is truly a vector which represents all the forces acting upon it.

The earth rotates at over 1,041 mph at the equator, so there is that momentum, but the earth's orbital speed and path around the sun means that the earth's more general path is in the direction of its orbit. As the earth's rotating surface would appear to a distant observer to be moving backwards from its direction of orbital motion over a period of a day, it is always moving toward its orbital path because its orbital speed (over 66,600 mph) is greater than its rotational speed. All the rotation does is periodically diminish and increase the speed of our "spot" on the earth's surface, and gradually rotate its orientation once every 24 hours, as it moves through space. With its compound movement and momentum---of the earth, the solar system, the Milky Way, etc.---we have a more complex pattern of movement, and since a body which is in constant, compound, gradual, ever-changing motion relative to the ether, some interesting effects are bound to be found. These effects are not, as

36

described by Newton's laws, due to an attractive force acting at a distance, through an empty space.

Due to the relatively gradual orbiting and rotating changes in respect to the earth's motion relative to the ether-field, a relatively small amount of "externally acting" force ("gravity") would have to be ever-present in order for Newton's laws to apply even on the purely descriptive level, except for the local ether phenomenon I will specify in further detail, which insures "force-free" perpetual motion, *despite* the gravitational effects. While I agree with that part of Einstein's theory that says gravity is not due to the direct action of one object to another, I disagree with the part that says it is due to the idea that a body "wraps" space around itself and "curves it". Without an ether, there is nothing to curve, and with it, there is no Relativity theory.

In early 1995, in exchange for a copy of *Space Aliens*, I received a copy of Eric Lerner's *The Big Bang Never Happened*, and was pleased to find there are some in the academic world of physics (or astrophysics), who share at least in part, my own views on the Big Bang Theory, although they don't go so far as I do in saying the theory was created and promoted by the coercive energy monopolists, because of its apparent intent to negate the free energy available from the ether, due to what I call the "Law of Conservation of Perpetual Motion". I also find Lerner's book refreshing, not to mention useful in charting some of my ideas on a more cosmic scale.

Lerner's unsung hero is Hannes Alfvén, a Norwegian astrophysicist and cosmographer, whose earlier "academic burial" by the Relativists was somewhat reversed in 1970 by a Nobel Prize awarded to him for his development of magneto-hydrodynamics and his concept of frozen lines of magnetic force, a theory later repudiated in part by Alfvén himself. Alfvén had in a way replaced the word "ether" with "plasma", and strongly disagreed with the Relativist's misuse of mathematical theory, which he said 'must always be the servant of physical understanding and close observation, rather than its master'. He claimed giant currents through space, from the sun through the planets, along magnetic lines of force, actually transfer angular momentum to the planets. This discovery, together with his work on cosmic MHD events, places Alfvén's work very close to Tesla's Dynamic Theory of Gravity.

The appearance of such books as Lerner's is a positive development, which represent dissent which seems intolerable to the Relativists. The Big Bang Theory is in decline among scientists, despite all the NASA false propaganda in the press and mass media attempting to perpetuate and support it. I recommend Lerner's book, even though he has not yet evoked an affirmative support for ether theory, but has dared to challenge Relativism and the Big Bang cosmology.

The actual course that a particular spot on earth takes through the universe is naturally more complex than that of the sun, since the earth represents a smaller cycle within the larger. Relative to the ether-field, the entire interrelated movements of the solar system and Milky Way takes our spot in a generally wavy path, along which our velocity relative to the ether periodically accelerates and decelerates.

The same principles of momentum which apply to the cosmos must also apply to the motion of immediately local bodies, except that the effects are skewered by the presence of earth's pesky electric, magnetic, and so-called "gravity" fields. What Alfvén had touch upon in his long-unrecognized discovery of giant electric and magnetic currents through space, are similar to unrecognized forces operative on a local scale as well. As our planet hurls through space at 70,000 mph, and us with it, there are things happening on a super-microscopic scale of utmost importance, which play all-important parts in this giant panorama.

The big question---the one which those who invented the Big Bang cosmography sought prematurely to put to rest---is how can everything stay in perpetual motion under the Relativist theory, without violating the law of conservation of energy...and thereby also refuting the Relativist theory? The still-born theories of Tesla were still knawing at their throats, along with those of Alfvén, so they wanted to obscure all truly competing theories, and enshrine themselves in the annals of science for all time. Their method was to fabricate a scenario in which one original giant explosion was the 'origin' from which all we see is but an effect which will eventually "run down", like a car which is out of gas.

The missing ideas are how universal processes are continually self-replenished. Through an interplay of natural strong and weak forces and matter, perpetual motion is conserved. Strong forces overcome weaker forces. Cosmic radiation travels through the ether, until it reacts with plasma, forming matter. When matter concentrates, its forces concentrate. In contact with other, less concentrated matter, stronger, cosmic forces within the space it occupies are unleashed, producing transmutations and eventually more cosmic radiation, which travels through space until absorbed and converted by plasma or other mass, into more mass or radiation of lower frequency, and the process continues, ad infinitum.

The rigid thinker must have a simplistic answer as to "where matter comes from", "where it is going", "what is the purpose of life", or "what keeps everything going", etc. Sometimes we must accept reality, and discard phony theories which attempt to give us a simplistic answer for what we either must admit that we just don't know, or should consider some questions too stupid to ask. The facts concerning the existence of universal matter, forces, vast distances, massive bodies and events, and perpetual motion, are irreducible primaries or "first laws" about reality, which we must accept before we can progress with answering particular questions related to the more useful aspects of existence.

Since the orbital speed of earth around the sun is greater than the speed of earth's rotation, our spot never moves "backward" relative to the ether. Since the orbital speed of the Milky Way is greater than the orbital speed of the solar system or rotational speed of the earth, our spot continues in a generally "wavy-wavy" path in which we accelerate and decelerate over a one-day short cycle, while the entire earth moves in a wavy path over a 365-day longer cycle, and so fourth. There are still larger and larger cycles of motion over time, in which the solar system orbits the Milky Way, the Milky Way orbits the Magellanic Clouds, and so on. As can be seen from these cyclical movement, the universe is an unlimited system of interrelated systems which move in gear-like precision, rather than in an *explosive* pattern *ala* the Big Bang. Universal movement is in an orderly, cyclical pattern of circles (or ellipses), within circles, representing mechanical oscillations which are related to smaller and larger electromagnetic ones. The exceptions to this---the occasional cosmic explosion, such as that of a supernova---are the exceptions which prove rather than disprove the rule. Even the occasional comet follows a cyclical pattern, while the debris from cosmic events eventually falls into patterns. Though such explosions on our scale are gigantic, they are like minor ripples in a pond on a cosmic scale, and should not be allowed to warp our perspective.

If last week a remote controlled telescope---such as the Hubbell---showed a movement which when compared to an earlier measurement of a few years ago indicated a movement away from a distant part of the universe, just remember that this is only an observation of movement which is part of a much larger pattern of oscillation over a much longer period of time, in which the movement will later appear to be going the other way, from our point of view, if we could make an observation millions of years or longer into the future. Because of the circuitous pattern of movement which we observe in relation to earth at the present, and the larger structures in "our vicinity" of the universe, we have good reason to believe that all such movements are cyclical, and to extrapolate ourselves into the time when the appearance would be quite different. The theory that the earth and other celestial bodies are the result of the Big Bang are ludicrous. The universe has no age, as it has always existed, and always will exist. The whole theory about how planets "were created" is erroneous.

Life forms would not only have to have existed at one time on Mars, but on all other planets and stars, at some time. In fact, the planets grew from smaller bodies as a result of life forms, which convert interstellar radiation into solid mass. There is no depth to which we can drill on earth, or otherwise produce direct evidence to the contrary, where we will not find matter which was in its past part of living things. This theory of course makes the planet "too old" for the Big Bangers, as it would take a much longer time to reach its present state, and would throw their "calendar"---on which the high priests of "Big Bangery" have placed the earth's "birth date"---off.

For example, one of the components of chlorophyll is iron. This iron along with carbon deposits and other elements results from photosynthesis. If strata of the earth, thousands of feet, even miles thick, are composed of the decayed and metamorphosed remains of plant and animal life, the original biomass represents a conversion ultimately of radiation through photosynthesis, and into the many elements and minerals composing the strata, which can be easily traced to this process, such as iron, calcium, phosphorus, sulfur, nitrogen, carbon, hydrogen, oxygen, and helium. Such elements accumulate through the cosmically-driven forces of life forms. There is probably a constant of universal mathematical proportionality between life forms and inorganic ones.

The ether, the medium which conducts the ZPR, can be converted into any form of matter or energy. It is possible to precipitate any element out of the ether, using proper technology. The ether contains the building blocks of what we call "solid matter", the proof of which enhances this possibility.

Nikola Tesla eventually realized the ether's use in his discovery of the "tremendous propelling force". His electropulsive technology works, and that is more important that splitting hairs...or atoms.

Only an ether which is intimately involved with momentum, could explain such a tremendous propulsion force such as that which I observed in 1953. This propulsive force was nothing more than a force which exists in nature, which in the hands of man becomes an article of will, once the physical processes capable of synthesizing and manipulating it become known.

From the rate and manner of acceleration, in conjunction with the probable mass of the ship I observed, it was immediately apparent that the entire volume of the ship, if filled with conventional rocket or jet fuel, would have been consumed in the three seconds required for it to accelerate to c.9,000 mph and disappear at infinity, except for the existence of Tesla's technology which electromagnetically canceled inertia and synthesized a new momentum instantaneously.

What is inertia? Inertia is the momentum which a body 'at rest' already possesses because it is in a state of uniform motion, but which to us appears to be at rest. Tesla's technology uses the electromagnetic interaction, which is 10^{40} times stronger than gravity, to create a "tremendous propelling force" which instantaneously reprograms the atoms and molecules of a ship with new micro helical tubes of force along a new trajectory, and destroys the " memory" of the tubes of force which created its prior inertia/momentum.

Electropulsion is a "free energy" process in which energy existing in the environment---"gravity" and momentum---are overcome by and replaced with the naturally stronger force of electromagnetism, to perform a greater amount of work during a given time, which theoretically is 10^{40} times more work, using a smaller amount of "input energy" to trigger the change. If "energy" is "the ability to do work", and "work" is the "movement of mass through a distance", then a stronger force will do more work over a given time period. A change of form of energy from a weaker to a stronger force (which exists in the environment) will use "environmental energy" to do more work in a new way.

The process which makes electropulsion possible, is the dynamism of the universe, which naturally exchanges weaker and stronger forces to conserve perpetual motion, with any lost momentum being resupplied by the ZPR.

CHAPTER III: OBSERVATIONS

With Tesla's theory and the background of older research and theories held temporarily in abeyance, let's look at what has been directly observed either by myself of by those closely associated with me.

What I began observing in 1946, and have continued ever since, are man-made electro-propulsive flying machines which can hover, turn on a dime at high speed without flying apart, and accelerate almost instantaneously to at least 9,000 mph, without readily audible sound or sonic boom. The ship I observed in 1953, in broad daylight, hovering at about 300 feet distance, about 250 feet above ground level, precessed at a high angle---about 45 degrees---and a low rate of about two precessions per second. Soon after I spotted it, it began to move away directly due west, quickly accelerating to about 800 mph, at which time it did two absolutely square turns---a right angle turn straight down and another right angle turn back to level flight---then accelerated to a point of infinity above the horizon in three seconds. The ship was constructed as if it were two 50-foot diameter stainless steel woks joined together clamshell fashion. It had concentric "striations"---grooves in its surface which appeared to be about one inch wide all over its surface---which gave its bottom half the appearance of a giant "spun-metal" wok, as it precessed with the sun's rays playing on its bright metallic surface. The sun was about ten degrees above the horizon at the time.

As it precessed, it gave off a sparkling, "rainbow-colored" electrical corona, like a metallic surface which was being electrified with high voltage Tesla currents. On the shadow side of the bottom away from the sun, as the ship precessed, there appeared a soft, 'cloudy', infra-red glow, which indicated the possible presence of microwaves, while the general "rainbow" corona was apparently of high voltage electricity. As the ship began accelerating, the rainbow corona formed a sparkling, scintillating trail behind the ship, which also showed a "texture" of lines in the trail which appeared to indicate the frequency of the pulses. Since the lines appeared to be "about" five feet apart at "about" 200 mph, the frequency could have been 60 cycles per second---a frequency which is very low, with the approx. 5-foot-spaced pulses coming at the quarter wavelength. This rough guess is based on what "200 m.p.h." looked like from our vantage point. (Note: In Tesla's time, "microwaves" were those of only a few feet or inches, such as those he measured coming from the earth during his 1899 Colorado Springs Experiments. The "internal" frequency possibly used with this ship---the penetrating long waves, oriented along the direction of acceleration, to polarize the "tubes of force" necessary for the propulsive force to act on the ether---were apparent from the outside, as the pulsing effect graphically illustrated by five-foot spaces left in the scintillating ion trail.

Consistent with the observed behavior, the electro-propulsive system appeared to instantly synthesize in an internal atomic way, inertia and momentum, things which normally create problems in acceleration and turning, but which the system overcame as shown by the evidence of the square, right angle turns. The system appeared to have very little to do with "gravity", even though it also revealed that gravity is apparently due to the same kinds of electromagnetic mechanisms. These observations were taken at face value, as proof of certain facts concerning the nature of the ether, gravity, inertia, momentum, and "electropulsion".

I had observed whole squadrons of saucers at night, between 1947-53, during which time I slept outdoors in our back yard. The squadrons arrived over our town from the direction of New Mexico (about ten miles from the southern New Mexico border), and departed back in that direction after their night-time maneuvers. (Note: The ship involved in the 1953 sighting flew due east, toward the northern tip of Ft. Bliss, near El Paso, Texas. Ft. Bliss was the location of Headquarters, U.S. Army Ordinance, where Wernher von Braun was appointed research director in the summer of 1945. The ordinance headquarters was subsequently moved, along with von Braun's main base of operation, to Redstone Arsenal, Alabama, about 1951.)

The night squadron saucers turned in angles of 30 degrees or multiples (30, 60, 90,120, 180, etc. degrees). That meant they had the same navigation and control system as the 1943-vintage German saucers which my Peiltochterkompass was used on.

My observations, together with all the written information on the Peiltochterkompass, and an analysis of the device itself, revealed quite a lot about the German "Kreisel Teller- p2" and its propulsion system:

1. The ships were electrically propelled;

2. The propulsion system created an electric field around the saucers which necessitated the development of an inertial guidance system and compass, since a magnetic compass would be useless due to the "Faraday cage" effect;

3. The ships were circular, discus-shaped craft, which turned in

43

twelve *peripheral* directions of the compass, plus "up" and "down";

4. The ships used a horizontally oriented master gyro-compass ("Meisterkreiselkompass"), calibrated prior to take-off to true north, as the frame of reference with which to navigate the ship using an electromagnetic slave compass, which was interconnected to stepping switches which also actuated the ship's bi-polar propulsion electrodes;

5. the system canceled the normal effects of gravity, inertia, and momentum, and instantly synthesized momentum in the chosen direction, without disturbing the operation of the master gyro, which continued to maintain its heading during flights, apparently because of an 'internal' inertia/momentum within the ship's outer shell;

6. the instant turns showed an incompressible ether which is integrally locked with mass in the phenomena of inertia, momentum, and gravity.

Since the 1953 daylight sighting, I have seen many other electropulsive craft, but one of the best sightings I made was on a moonlit night while soaking in a hot tub.

Rub-a-Dub-Dub, Seven Folks in a Hot Tub

On a Wednesday evening, January 24, 1996, at approximately 7:00 PM, I sat in a hot tub with seven other people, at the *Ten Thousand Waves Japanese Bath House,* located on the western slopes of the Sangre de Christos Mountains, in the Hyde Park vicinity above Santa Fe, New Mexico. As I steamed in the tub, conversation between a couple from Denver and myself drifted from the dangers of fluoride to "What do you do?", to which I answered, "I write some". Asked what I had written, I answered "A book called Space Aliens from the Pentagon."

A beautiful woman on my right exclaimed "I have your book. I'm a friend of Alex and Rex. I love your book so much, and so do they." I thanked her and we exchanged introductions, and then I said, "I see saucers up here almost every time I'm here after dark...and as a matter of fact, there's one right there" (pointing out a flashing aircraft flying slowly easterly about 15 degrees to the lower left of the crescent moon, at a distance of about 10,000 feet from us).

A heckler across the tub said "Aww, that's a plane", to

which I responded, "There's another one...and if they're planes, why have they parked? The flashing lights mask an underlying glow. The eye recoils from a flash, and never has time to recover before another flash. When they move faster, they glow brighter, which is why they are going so slowly."

No sooner had I spoken, than the stationary ship on the left quit flashing, and turned into a dark, glowing green shape like a football field surrounded by a track. Around the "track" was a dark strip, with a purple corona outside that, produced by the Tesla coils. I could see the curvature of its bottom as it moved, flying in a large circle, as I followed it with my outstretched arm and index finger, and my fellow hot-tubbers oggled in jaw-dropped amazement. The following is a black-and-white photo of a painting I did of the saucer, as seen from the bottom:

It returned to its starting point, skidded to a halt, and began flashing again. This took approximately ten seconds. Since the ship appeared about one-half to three-quarters of an inch at arm's length (about 2 feet), at the 10,000-foot distance, it was around 400 feet long and 250 feet wide. Since the diameter of the circle from top to bottom was about 30 degrees, its speed was about 2,000 miles per hour (the speed didn't surprise me, since I clocked the one I saw in 1953 over our back yard at minimum of 9,000 mph when it departed). I almost missed it, because I didn't have my glasses, and because it appeared to have been "stealth-ized"---designed to be concealed by the night sky, by controlling its emissions to be a dark green and purple, so as to more closely match the light value and blend into the night sky. The main 'give-away' was the color differences.

Others in the tub---most of whom didn't need glasses---saw it more sharply than I, yet wouldn't have seen it at all if I had not pointed it out to them. I probably would not have seen it myself, had I not been observing the flashing ships beforehand, with the moon so close above, creating some back-lighting which helped to define the darker silhouette when it developed. Moreover, the real reason I saw it, was my own preconscious mental self-conditioning.

I was amazed at its large size, since, when flashing, it appeared much smaller. When I finally looked back to the other side of the tub, the heckler was gone, the on-cue saucer demo being apparently too much for him. If the saucer crew had been listening to my words, their performance couldn't have been more perfectly timed. Bravo! Do they also have some computer software that reads lips? It is my theory that the government jerks have chosen that particular location to do some "testing", because of the titillating availability of the numerous private hot tubs open to the night sky, occupied by private nude couples of all sexual persuasions, ready to be video taped by them. I can just see them trading the tapes among themselves, another good reason to "...keep the secret", to avoid prosecution.

It was the first time I had seen the green-glowing type reported years ago by astronomer Clyde Tombaugh, discoverer of the planet Pluto. It was the second most graphic demonstration of saucer technology I have witnessed. If I had not spotted it, none of us would have seen anything extraordinary, excluding the beautiful lady next to me who liked my book, and was a strong competition to the saucers. Incidentally, the female breast shape may be "natures most nearly-perfect shape for a flying saucer design". Hmmm...maybe the "cigar-shaped" ships were dreamed up by a woman. The "green-glowing" type was apparently the result of research designed to make the ships less visible in the night sky, since the early models---such as the "foo-fighters" ("Fliegende Schildkrote" ["Flying Turtle"] and "Kugelblitz" ["Ball Lightning"]) glowed brightly. The oblong design (as distinguished from the circular or 'peripheral' saucers) comports with what I call the "linear type" in my book. According to a friend who is an expert spectrographer, the green corona indicated atomic absorption, which I presume to be 'stealth' technology used to suppress the white light spectrum. He seemed to think sodium based coating, while I think maybe chromium, because it appeared to be a veridian ("chrome") green. The soft, 'cloudy' green also indicated positive corona, as distinguished from the 'hairy' negative (purple) corona around the outer periphery.

Comparison to Other Sightings

The hot tub sighting was not a clear, "daylight", "close-range" sighting, like the first good sighting which I had personally made on a bright, late summer afternoon in West Texas, in 1953, within 300 feet, right over our back yard, in Kermit, Texas, as our family and friends were having an ice cream party. I had been the last in my family and neighborhood to see a saucer in a close-up daylight sighting, since three had appeared on two consecutive days, June 1st and 2nd 1950, while I was unfortunately in the Davis Mountains about 120 miles to the west. My father has seen more of them than I, and was once held in his car for 15-30 minutes, on the night of Nov. 2, 1957, just south of Levelland, Texas, by one of the 200-foot-long, egg-shaped chingas, which had scared the livin' daylights out of him. The thing hovered within ten feet of his car top, killed his engine, and burned out all his lights, yet failed to burn out a single fuse in any of the car's circuits. The saucer's electric field was so strong that it arrested current flow, and was strong enough to cancel the magnetic fields in the generator and circuits. The white-hot tungsten filaments were the weakest points in the circuits, and the saucer's pulse currents apparently subjected them to magnetic and electric shear forces which broke them apart.

My father had to drive back to Levelland in the dark, spend the night in a motel, then drive home to Odessa, Texas at dawn's first light. He arrived home about 7:00 AM, had a quick breakfast, and left for Sewell Ford to have his lights fixed, saying nothing about the saucer. I turned on the TV for the morning news as he left, and realized that he had been one of the several drivers held by the ship (or ships) that night. I drove to Sewell Ford, and questioned him about it as the mechanic fixed the lights. He asked how I knew about it, and I told him it was on the news. He said he didn't want to be called "crazy". This was what I call "anti-paranoia". It was reasonable to fear ridicule created by government propaganda.

Later, in 1963, I had the opportunity to discuss the matter more fully with the sheriff of Hockley County, while working in Brownfield, Texas, as a graphic artist, doing advertising art for a manufacturing and publishing operation which had contact with the soil conservation district with which the sheriff was affiliated. The ship seen by my father matched in shape, appearance, and performance, the type observed by deputy Lonnie Zamora, near Soccorro, New Mexico. Zamora had at first described the crew of the ships as typical G.I.s in grey-green Air Force jump suits, but later altered his story, saying they were "...about the size of children". This was after the security spooks 'leaned' on him.

Saucers can be seen almost any night in the area where I live, and are very profuse in an even more obvious way around the Cheyenne Mountain area to the south of Colorado Springs, where the underground NORAD complex is located. With the several direct observations, or reports from those in my family or from my close friends as "proof of the pudding" kept firmly in mind, let's see what more can be found in ether theory history to reflect on them.

The Ether and "Ponderable Matter"

In 1879, James Clerk Maxwell (1831-1879) said that the velocity of the solar system relative to the ether could be determined by observing the retardation of the eclipses of Jupiter's satellites. The observed behavior---in which the light of a star can be viewed with a steady image as the earth moves through space---indicates a stationary ether relative to a moving earth, solar system, and other bodies. The ether is ultrafine, yet very dense, and composed of positive and negative electric matter, which pervades all so-called "free space", as well as the space "occupied"

48

by "mass"---which the old ether physicists called "ponderable matter"---because it is mostly "space". Since the ether is stationary, it is the 'ponderable bodies' which move through it, just as Fresnel said, rather than vice-versa.

The ether is transparent, because of its ultra fine, high frequency structure, which does not refract or reflect visible light, because its ultra-fine size is too tiny to react to such low frequency radiation. To momentively "access" the ether in a propulsive way, high voltage pulses are required. This is in accord with J.J. Thomson's "electromagnetic momentum" theory, and was confirmed by the tests conducted by Nikola Tesla by 1891 (later detailed in his 1891 lecture before the A.I.E.E., Columbia College, N.Y.). Tesla's tests confirmed a reaction which was more than the feeble ionic reaction of light gases such as the misinformational 1950's "patents" of T. Townsend Brown later attempted to induce the gullible public to believe was the correct technology. After his tests, Tesla stated that the ether became a 'solid state' medium to "light and heat" (visible and infrared light), and could be accessed by subjecting it to "sufficiently high voltage and frequency".

The ether becomes more apparent when there is a sudden change in the *direction of motion, rate of acceleration, or velocity* of a body. The movement of a charged body, equivalent to a current, creates a new degree of electrical displacement of the ether through which it moves, and influences the resistance to changes in velocity through the affected ether by the protons and electrons composing the body itself. The increased work required to move the sphere---caused by an increased "resistance" called "inertia", must be reflected by the increase in its tendency to remain in motion which is called "momentum", which demonstrates a rearrangement of the manner of movement of or displacement of the positive and negative charges which correspond to the motion. Therefore, once in motion at a constant velocity, though a charged body requires more conventional work to set it in that motion, its momentum would be increased by the increased charges, consistent with an increase of its "virtual mass". It is clear that both inertia and momentum are caused by the same thing, which is a persistence by the configuration of reaction patterns in the atomic and electric structure of mass to maintain their present states. Just as changing magnetic fields or electric fields are required for inductance, the creation of such changing fields by changing motion are the basis for inertia and momentum.

All bodies are in motion, and within all bodies, protons and electrons are also in motion, because "elasticity" and vibratory motion occurs in "ponderable matter" and in the ether. The ether sets up certain patterns of motion in the electrons and protons (and atoms and molecules) in ponderable matter passing through it.

As the earth passes through the ether, its rapidly varying electrostatic forces reach out for some distance and polarize the negative electrical components of the ether, and affects bodies within its reach, creating what we call "gravity".

The stationary ether, appearing to move through an earth-bound body, due to the earth's motion through it, undergoes a change in electrical displacement, due to the difference in dielectric constant between the space outside the body and the space within the body. The electrical displacement in the ether outside the body prior to entry, and the electrical displacement as it enters and passes through the body, changes due to the change in dielectric constant, and affects the "electric content" (protons and electrons, electric charges and fields, and magnetic fields) within the body. These changes in turn cause the changes in electric displacement of the ether---a downward thrust on the body's atoms, away from the pre-existing "equilibrium position", which the atoms would occupy in the absence of gravity---just as Maxwell said. The "equilibrium position" for the electrical particles of ponderable matter vary according to the dielectric constant. A change in dielectric constant results in a change in the equilibrium position, through an electric displacement, which eventually may result in a new equilibrium position. The time-relative aspect of gravity is due to the inertia of a falling body at any stage of its fall, which forces the gradual increase in pitch of its micro helical tubules.

In summary, inside an earth-bound body at rest relative to the earth, there is a difference in polarization and displacement effects, from those which exist outside the body in free space. Since earth's electric field is graduated through the intermediate space, between the negative at earth's surface, and the positive at the ionosphere, the dielectric properties are subjected to graduated strains. The effects of electrical displacement and gravity vary accordingly, somewhat like Newton's "inverse square" law. It is here that a difference between the "force of gravity" and the effects of inertia and momentum become apparent.

Traditionally, inertia has always been considered (according to Newton's *First Law of Motion*) the tendency of a body "at rest" or in "constant velocity" relative to the earth, to continue its state of rest or constant velocity, unless acted upon by an external force. Since all bodies at rest relative to the earth are already moving at the same "constant velocity" of the earth however, only *changes in movement* relative to the earth are at issue, and any such changes affect the patterns of flow within mass of the tubes of force, as it moves through the ether, at any given time. Since only a body which moves in respect to the earth has been traditionally said to have "momentum" ("the product of a body's mass and velocity"), this rule is wrong, since all bodies "at rest" relative to earth already have "momentum" as well as "inertia".

Momentum and inertia are due to the exact same "tendency", which relates ultimately to a frame of reference to the universal ether, but for convenience---since we don't have an absolute "fix" on the ether yet---we use the moving earth as a frame of reference from which to measure a body's *rate of change* relative to the ether, as the earth maintains its relatively constant velocity. There is a special case on earth, because the ether within the reach of earth's electric field has been "conditioned"---that is, its dielectric constant has been subjected to electric strain. This comports with Tesla's statements concerning the effects of "rapidly varying electrostatic forces" emanating from earth.

The earth has momentum within the sun's frame of reference, just as a moving car has momentum within the earth's frame of reference. Some physicists have mistakenly applied a "field of influence' idea, thinking this "field of gravitational influence" somehow isolates a body from references outside this field. I believe that earth's "gravitational field" is a product of its moving electric field (a "current") as it influences the ether within it, and that the so-called "gravity field" extends no further than earth's electric field.

Momentum is due to the setting up inside a body, of micro helical tubular vibrations of atomic structures, composed of electrical particles---electrons and protons---as the body passes through the ultra fine ether. The micro helical rotation of these tubules are the product of the *magnetic rotation of the plane of polarization* identified by Faraday. Any variance from earth's uniform motion results in a resistance to change in micro helical pitch, since the rotating tubes of force spin around so much of the irrotational ether cores ("Onmi") over a given period of time, and a change in motion requires them to rotate around a commensurately greater or lesser quantity of Omni, depending on whether the change is an acceleration or deceleration. The tubules possess electromagnetic force which is locked into the discrete flow pattern between the Omni and the tubules, which are coupled to the 'ponderable matter' structure which is the recipient of the momentum. It is probable that the linkage between matter and the ether is effected by a current—perceived as "electric charge"— which passes through the matter constantly at a rate which is commensurate to the relative velocity difference.

Though the flow patterns of the microhelical tubules are always gradually changing—because of the continual reorientation of the earth as it moves in its "uniformly compound" changing ways, these changes are sensually imperceptible because they are gradual over time, with effects which are virtually constant. Though the changes are too slow to sense, the action of the tides is probably related to them.

The natural gravity force is always normally toward the earth, which is negatively charged, within earth's electric/gravity field, due to the polarity of that field, since the negative component of the ether in free space is electrically displaced upward by the repulsion of like charges, while the inertial characteristics of the more massive positive component is forced and attracted downward, and is more resistant to changes in displacement. As the ether enters a body at rest on earth, its displacement changes because of the change in dielectric constant, just as Maxwell said. As the dielectric constant of the body changes, the electric displacement of the ether within the entrained atomic structure of the body changes, creating a downward force as each of the negative electrical components of the ether move downward, creating an increased attractive force on protons above, and an increased repulsive force on electrons below.

The moving ether particles create the gravity force, similar to how an inverted aerodynamic airfoil creates a down-force on an airplane. Due to the greater velocity of the electromagnetic interaction at C however, this down-force is irrespective to the direction of earth's movement relative to the ether, since the interaction between the electrical components of matter and the ether at C, is due to the conditioning of the ether by earth's electric field, which is vertically polarized, and creates the same proximate effect on mass over time, irrespective as to earth's orientation relative to the ether. Though the velocity of earth relative to the ether is thousands of miles per hour, it is not fast enough to "outrun" the electromagnetic interaction.

Orbiting Planets and Satellites

The concept that a satellite in orbit around earth is "held" in orbit by "earth's field of gravity", seems false. The logical implication of my analysis is that the orbital path taken by a body is because it "sees" that path as one of least resistance, *as if it were a straight and level path.* Since for a given radius above earth the ether is displaced to a certain degree, an orbiting body would experience an accelerating force which would be met by inertia, if it were to move upward, and a decelerating force which would be met by momentum, if it were to move downward, so its path in force-free constant velocity remains at a constant radius or level of etheric displacement, as the path of least resistance.

Since the determinative factor which limits a body's motion is the reactance of its internal electrical content with the ether at its particular degree of displacement by earth's electric field, at a given altitude, an orbiting body "sees" its orbital path along a path of like displacement, as a straight and level path, even though it is a straight and orbiting path. This path is rather concentric to the earth at a certain altitude. This is similar to how Einstein said that *space and time* are "wrapped" around a large spinning body as it moves through space, except Einstein believed in no ether, without which "empty space" would have nothing to "wrap".

One of the revealing facts obviated by films of astronauts floating in the so-called "gravity-free" space of an orbiting space station, is the contradictory assertion that the space station is "held" in orbit by earth's gravity. If the earth's gravity exerted sufficient force to hold the station in orbit, the internal environment would not be "gravity free", but would pull the astronauts down to the floor, instead of allowing them to float all around inside, as we've seen so many times on TV. Yet, there is sufficient elasticity within the internal masses of the astronauts' bodies, between electrical content and the ether, to allow movement in that manner. Maxwell said this elasticity resides in the magnetic fields.

CHAPTER IV: HISTORICAL DEVELOPMENT OF THE·THEORY

Rotatory Motion and the "Screw Effect"

Wm. Thomson (Lord Kelvin) first asserted that magnetism possesses a "rotatory" character related to heat or the thermal motions of a body (Proc. R.S. viii [1856], p. 150). Nikola Tesla made many references to Wm. Thomson, pointing to his work as a prelude to his own discoveries and applications which especially intensified in 1892. A review of the work of the world's major minds leading up to Tesla's breakthrough is necessary to show just what Tesla discovered and what it meant in respect to ether physics and physics in general.

Around 1870, Thomson had conducted experiments which seemed to indicate that "gravitational action" could be induced by spheroidal bodies oscillated by electrical currents or mechanical pulses (F. Guthrie Phil. Mag. xli [1871], p. 405). The surface pulsations could cause attractions or repulsions in respect to other bodies, as verified by Thomson. Tesla was aware of Thomson's work during his student days in Graz, Austria, beginning 1875, when he was 19. Thomson's work undoubtedly served as the spark of inspiration for Tesla in his early conception of an "ideal flying machine" which would be propelled by electricity acting upon the ether. This explains Tesla's continual references to Thomson, such as demonstrating during his 1892 London lecture, a 'luminous wire' sign powered by a Tesla coil, which said "WILLIAM THOMSON".

At first, Thomson found that ponderomotive forces act between two solid bodies immersed in an incompressible fluid, when one of the bodies is immobilized and made to oscillate with a force which acts along a line between its center and that of a much larger sphere which is free. The free sphere was attracted to the smaller (immobilized) sphere, if its density was greater than the fluid, while a sphere of less density than the fluid was repelled or attracted, according to the ratio of its distance to the vibrator in relation to a certain quantity (Phil. Mag. xli [1871], p. 405; Letter, Thomson to F. Guthrie, p. 427.)

Thomson's experiments were analogical ones, for which he had evoked praise from his contemporaries even when he was still a teenager, although his refusal to believe anyone's assertions unless he could build an analogical model to prove them often led to the consternation of those of his contemporaries, such as Maxwell, who relied often on mathematical equations. The sphere experiments were designed to use mechanical and electrical wave methods to construct a model to probe the gravitational, inertial and momentive reactions of solid bodies in the ether.

The Faraday effect---the rotation of the plane of polarization of radiation in a dielectric medium (such as the atmosphere, space, and certain solid materials) in a magnetic field---stated that the angle of rotation of radiation is proportional to the magnetic field strength and the length of the path in the medium in the field. These early experimenters knew there was a connection between the rotatory motion and momentum, and sought to find it.

The rotatory (versus the linear) character of magnetic phenomena was strengthened by Thomson's experimentally verified conclusions on the magnetic rotation of light. This rotatory character not only influenced Tesla's discovery of the rotating magnetic field, but is also fundamental to inertia and momentum, as I will later explain, since movement of a charged body constitutes a current which creates a magnetic field which creates the rotatory motion which "bores" through the ether like a drill to create momentum.

Thomson's system was later investigated by C.A. Bjerknes between 1877 and 1910. Bjerknes showed that when two spheres immersed in an incompressible fluid were pulsated, they exerted a mutual attraction which obeyed Newton's inverse square law if the pulsations were in phase, while if the phases differed by a half wave, the spheres repelled. At one quarter wave difference, there was no action. Where pulses were non-instantaneous at distances greater than a quarter wavelength, attractions and repulsions were reversed (Repertorium d. Mathematik I [Leipzig, 1877], p. 268; Proc. Camb. Phil. Soc. iii [1879], p. 276; iv [1880], p. 29).

The publishings of these researches and experiments in the physical journals of Europe were available to Nikola Tesla, during his student days at the Polytechnic Institute in Graz, Austria, and at the University of Prague, in Czechoslovakia. Tesla could read and understand all these pertinent journals in their original languages.

Around 1878, George Francis FitzGerald (1851-1901) (Phil Trans. clxxi [1880], p. 691; FitzGerald's Scientific Writings, p. 45) compared magnetic force and velocity in a quasi-elastic solid, based on a model devised earlier by James MacCullagh (1809-47) (Brit. Assoc. Rep., [1835]), whose model was the only one which could propagate waves

55

with the properties of light---obviously analogous to the electromagnetic theory of light---as shown by MacCullagh's ether equation of motion and ether theory which made it feasible to extend ether concepts to represent optical phenomena, along with magnetic and electric interaction.

An Electrostatic Charge Carried Around

In 1879, Edwin H. Hall (<u>Amer</u>. <u>Jour</u>. <u>Math</u>. ii [1879], p. 287) a student in Baltimore, repeated an experiment suggested by H. A. Rowland, his professor, whose original experiment with a gold-foil-covered ebonite disk in a magnetic field showed that electric charges on a disk were carried around with it as it was rotated (<u>Ann</u>. <u>d</u>. <u>Phys</u>, clviii [1876], p. 487). In Hall's experiment, a gold leaf strip in which a current was flowing, was placed into a magnetic gap. This produced an electromotive force at right angles to the magnetic field and the current, which was proportional to the product of the two. Called the "Hall Effect", it was already inherent in the three previous effects discovered much earlier by Faraday.

Faraday had discovered induction, by forcing a conductor through a magnetic field, cutting the lines of magnetic force and producing a current in the conductor. The second of Faraday's triad was production of a magnetic field in an unmagnetized iron core, by forcing a current-carrying conductor through a gap between the poles of a core. Faraday's third effect was the generation of a current. Though Hall's effect was inherent in the fact that it was the reverse of the force required by Faraday to push the conductor through a magnetic field, Hall's work completed the triad of effects, by bringing it into consciousness. This effect is the basis for MHD (Magneto-Hydrodynamic) generators, and electropropulsion, through the special means which would finally be brought into fruition by the work of Tesla.

Since the galvanometer needle in Hall's experiment was deflected only when the magnetic field arose or collapsed, the physical thrust created was a vector product which had already been expressly suggested in Maxwell's <u>Treatise</u> (1862), almost 15 years earlier (derived from Maxwell's analysis relative to Faraday's work of c. 1845), though Maxwell failed to follow up with experiment (because he died), the equations are still used.

Though it was said by Whittaker that the Hall effect, like the magnetic rotation of light, occurs only in ponderable bodies and not in the "free ether", this statement was patently false, since the effect actually depends on the conductivity of a medium. This was a definite lie on Whittaker's part, probably "required" under the 1951 revision. The fact that the effect occurs in "ponderable bodies" and "conductive media" however, is all-important for electropropulsion, since it shows the reaction between such bodies and media and the underlying "etheric framework" which is accessed in the process.

Since the "natural media" (the ether and the atmosphere) so often referred to by Tesla in his patents become conductive under the influence of electromagnetic radiation of sufficiently high voltage and frequency, the effects in the free ether, dependent upon proper conditions, can affect the ether within a ponderable body, so as to move the body through the free ether. The most startling proof that the Hall effect works in the free ether, was Tesla's "transmission" of electrical energy through space by high frequency oscillations, as detailed in his 1892 Lecture before the Institute of Electrical Engineers, London.

Since an electric field 'displaces' the ether---which is the basis for MHD pumping (especially when pulsed)---the effect actually showed an operable "electromotive force" ("emf"), or "electro-propulsive force", between ponderable bodies and the ether, by means of electromagnetic action. The high voltage and high frequency are required by the ether's great density and ultra-fineness. The moment Tesla had succeeded in *transmitting* electrical energy by means of high voltage, high frequency currents---"radio waves"---the ether was "accessed". Tesla's work at that point had already verified experimentally everything that Maxwell had mathematically analyzed as being the electromagnetic nature of light.

Though it was strongly implied, the literature available to me failed to explicitly state the idea that inertia and momentum are the products of an electromagnetic <u>rotatory</u> force which acts within bodies, upon a dense, incompressible ether which permeates all bodies and all space. Neither was it specified that a pulsating sphere or other ponderable body can be electrically propelled through the ether, without the presence of another sphere or other ponderable body to pull against---except in the statements of Nikola Tesla and his "flivver"/"model T" electropulsive "ideal electric flying machine".

In 1884, the year Tesla discovered the rotating magnetic field, J.J. Thomson attempted to determine the field produced by a moving electrified sphere, and the mathematical development of Maxwell's theory accelerated. It was naturally easier to solve such problems from the known behaviors of simple geometric forms---planes, spheres, and cylinders (J.J. Thomson, <u>Proc.</u> <u>Lond.</u> <u>Math.</u> <u>Soc.</u> xv [1884], p. 197).

The possibility that the ether was composed of stationary positive charges carrying their own 'sub-electronic' negative charges which were elastic, and could be displaced, had apparently evaded the thinking of Thomson. Although he had assumed that displacement currents must occur in the ether, he had earlier thought this was due to the magnetic effects of moving charges, though he failed to show how the displacement currents occurred, or what their effects were in terms of inertia and momentum.

There was already a sort of battle brewing between the proponents of classical electrodynamics, and the proponents led by Maxwell of an electromagnetic theory of light. To the former, conductivity occurred in metal wires, etc., while with Maxwell, it occurred in the surrounding dielectrics and ether-filled space, with the conductors serving only to "guide" the action. Tesla appeared to fit more into the Faraday/Maxwell camp. FitzGerald had unified the two views by arguing validly that Maxwell's unification was valid because radiation could be generated by purely electrical means.

Along this line, Thomson (1884) first considered a charged sphere moving uniformly in a straight line. He assumed that the electric charges were uniformly distributed, with an electric field the same in all directions, no matter what position the sphere was in, the same as if it were at rest. This assumption proved true so long as the velocity of the sphere and the velocity of light were neglected.

In 1889, Wm. Thomson (<u>Proc.</u> <u>Roy.</u> <u>Irish</u> <u>Acad.</u> i [30 Nov. 1889], p. 340), stated, "Rotational vortex-cores must be discarded; and we must have nothing but irrotational revolution and vacuous cores." By this, Thomson meant that the vacuous "ether", inside rotating tubes of electromagnetism, did not rotate, presumably because of its density, but also because, if the cores rotated along with the rotating tubes of electromagnetic force, it would neutralize the electro-mechanical action by which momentum is created.

FitzGerald found a purported error in Thomson's work, saying that the required "circuital condition" was not satisfied unless the moving charges on the sphere were considered as current, combined with the displacement and convection currents due to the motion. In correcting Thomson's error, FitzGerald went overboard in concluding that the magnetic force due to the displacement currents of the moving sphere, had no resultant effect. In this conclusion, FitzGerald seemed to have forgotten the "Faraday cage" and "magneto-optical" effects, since a moving charged sphere would constitute a current by his own admission, and all currents create magnetic fields, which cause the rotation of electromagnetic radiation and light in the surrounding ether as a resultant effect.

In 1888, Oliver Heaviside showed that the electrostatic and electromagnetic units "vanished" inside the sphere. This was the opposite to Faraday's experiment in which electrostatic charges placed inside a stationary, closed vessel, "appeared" on the outside. Apparently, movement of the sphere---which increases its momentum---appeared to Heaviside to force the charges back inside. Heaviside's conception of the "spherical" symmetry of charges during movement was disproved by G.C.F. Searle in 1896 (Phil. Trans. clxxxvii [1896], p. 675). Searle found that a moving "point charge" system is not a sphere, but an *oblate spheroid*, with a polar axis along its direction of motion. What Whittaker failed to point out, was the importance of this finding, a connection between inertia, momentum, current, surface charges "vanishing" and "reappearing", and an electromagnetic polarity along the direction of momentum, as well as an electro-mechanical link to the ether, since the displacement of the electric lines and polarity correspond to the movement, consistent to my thinking that the tubules create momentum inside a moving body. The "vanishing" electrostatic/electromagnetic units are 'occupied' internally by the microhelices, in perpetuating the movement of the body through the ether.

During this time, Nikola Tesla had not tarried. He had already shown that the "circuitous condition" could be met in a totally new way. In his lecture before the A.I.E.E. at Columbia College, N.Y., May 20, 1891, he demonstrated his years-old technology, and stated that he connected "one terminal" to a lamp and the other to "an insulated body of the required size. In all cases the insulated body serves to give off the energy into the surrounding space, and is *equivalent to a return wire*." In this lecture, Tesla also demonstrated "electromagnetic momentum" which J.J. Thomson was accredited with discovering in 1893 (J.J. Thomson, Recent Researches in Elect. And Mag., [1893],p. 13).

In the same year as Searle's finding (1896), W.B. Morton (Phil. Mag. xli [1896], p. 488) similarly showed that the surface density of a charged body is unaltered by motion, but the lines of force no longer leave the surface perpendicularly. He also found that the energy of the surrounding field is greater when in motion than when at rest. Since greater work is required to create a given velocity for a charged sphere, than for an uncharged one, and since the sphere can even move in a way which lessens the work, a connection between moving charges and an ether was verified. This was considered true because the charges increased the "virtual mass" of the sphere, and the self-induction of convection currents is formed when the charges are set in motion by movement of the sphere, but neither of these explanations seemed to explicitly note that a force between a moving charged mass and the space through which it moves must have an ether framework to push or pull against, or that a current is caused to flow between matter and the ether due to the movement.

J. Larmor (Phil. Trans. clxxxvi [1895], p. 697) suggested that the inertia of ponderable matter may be ultimately proven to be of this nature, since atoms were constituted of systems of electrons. The only objection to this was an inconsistency with the alleged "indivisibility" of the electron. This "indivisibility" I believe is due to a deceptive "apparent effect", produced by measuring instruments which measure only "whole" electrons, because they use only "whole protons", rather than ether particles. An "undivided electron" is the "equal and opposite" response to a "whole" positive charge. This is similar to Werner Heisenberg's "uncertainty principle", in that exact measurement of less than a whole electron is made impossible by the instruments of measurement.

If a greater "virtual mass" effect (W.B. Morton, supra) is created electrically, which increases or decreases the ease of movement of a body through the "free ether", and increases the total energy of the moving system, then a link between ponderable bodies and the etheric framework was proven, and the means for creating the imbalance of forces necessary for electro-propulsion---the use of moving charges in a specific way to synthesize the currents of a moving system---was just a matter of time and money for Nikola Tesla.

There were implications in the works of Faraday, Maxwell, Wm. Thomson, J.J. Thomson, MacCullagh, Morton, Searle, Heaviside, Hall, and FitzGerald, of a distinct relationship between momentum and the movement of charges connected to mass, through an interpenetrating gaseous, dynamic, neutral, ultra-fine ether existing in all space and ponderable matter, upon which electromagnetic ponderomotive forces act. Once the equilibrium of the ether and ZPR was "disturbed" by the moving system, the 'displacement' could be rectified only by an equal and opposite reaction, which was a flow of current between the moving system and the ether. Thomson had accepted the principle that the ether itself is the vehicle of mechanical momentum. The Hall effect had shown that an electromotive thrust is produced along a third axis as a result of a current and magnetic field at right angles, and though it was alleged that this thrust could not be produced "in the free ether", but only in ponderable matter, the works of Heaviside, Searle, and Morton showed that the moving charges could either increase or decrease the normal ease of movement of a body, proving the feasibility for electro-propulsion.

Since electrical processes are reversible, Tesla's method consisted of using Hall's MHD method to cause a flow of current between a 'stationary' system (relative to earth) and the ether---as if it were a "dynamic" system---since it mimicked the currents of a moving system, and created a disturbance in the ether which could only be rectified by movement of the system. Once the current commenced to flow, the magnetic fields thus created, imparted the rotatory force which created the micro helical tubes of force which 'drilled' their way around the irrotational ether cores, and synthesized the momentum which propelled the system through the ether.

Nikola Tesla's statement (<u>Lecture</u> <u>before</u> <u>the</u> <u>Institute</u> <u>of</u> <u>Immigrant</u> <u>Welfare</u>, May 12, 1938), that he had his *Dynamic Theory of Gravity* "all worked out" by 1893, and some 'available' documentation of Tesla's work of 1891 or earlier shows that he was already ahead of the European field led by J.J. Thomson, Searle, Morton, and Larmor, whose statements dated from the later 1890's.

As for his 1915 progress, Tesla stated in a Dec. 8, 1915 *New York Times* article that his electro-propulsive "...manless airship..." would travel "...300 miles a second..." (1.08 million mph), "...without propelling engine or wings, sent by electricity to any desired point on the globe...".

The Sept. 22, 1940 *New York Times* article by Wm. L. Laurence completed the documentation, by stating that Tesla had already tested his four-part *Teleforce* system, which included "...a new method for producing a tremendous electrical <u>propelling</u> force...", as used on his electrical aircraft.

CHAPTER V: TESLA AND THE GOOD OLD BOYS' CLUB

When Tesla popped into the picture, the British "Good Old Boy's Club" had been debating ether theory for quite some time, and the upstart Tesla must have hurt the pride of their linemen, by making an end run to make a touchdown.

In 1847, W. Thomson, in discussing the motion of a magnetizable body in a non-uniform field of force, said a charged body attracts a body having a greater specific inductive capacity than that of the surrounding medium, and repels a body with a lower specific inductive capacitance, to afford the path of best conductance to the lines of force.

Thomson had also stated that an electrode immersed in a fluid insulating medium (an experimental analogy to a body in ether-filled space), at "...sufficiently high frequency", would cause a gravitation of gases all around toward the electrode, but that the general opinion (of he and his European colleagues) was that it was "out of the question" that such frequencies could be reached. This last opinion was soon to be disproved by a close follower **and** admirer of Thomson's work.

In reiteration, another Thomson---J.J. Thomson---had claimed to have mathematically developed the theory of moving tubes of force (<u>Phil. Mag.</u> xxxi [1891], p. 149). For his *Recent Researches in Electricity and Magnetism* (1893, p. 13), his hypothesis was the "the aether is a storehouse of mechanical momentum", but was this correct? Isn't it more likely that the "storehouse" of "mechanical momentum" is in "ponderable matter" which reacts with the ether?

Nikola Tesla's lecture before the A.I.E.E. at Columbia College in 1891 was based on earlier experiments. He mentioned the "tubes of force" and disclosed some of his discoveries concerning ether and momentum. His Feb., 1892 lecture before the Institute of Electrical Engineers, London, at a time when the Good Old Boys were still debating whether an electromagnetic action could occur in the free ether, Tesla explained he planned to run motors at a distance by wireless energy, with equipment he had already built, and to extract free energy from the environment.

Four years later, Wm. Thomson stated his "inclination" to "speculate" that "alterations of electrostatic force due to rapidly changing electrification" are propagated by "condensational waves in the luminiferous aether" (Bottomley, <u>Nature</u> liii [1896], p. 268). This seemed to indicate that Thomson was just beginning to take Tesla seriously.

In his 1892 London lecture for the Good Old Boys, Tesla had stated that the 'required' frequencies--- which Thomson had said were "out of the question" to be produced---were "...much lower than one is apt to estimate at first", and continued (in pertinent part, emphasis mine): "We may cause the molecules of the gas to collide by the use of alternate electric impulses of high frequency, and so we may imitate the process of a flame; and from experiments with high frequencies which we are now able to obtain, I think the result is producible with impulses which are transmissible through a conductor." "...it appeared to me of great interest to demonstrate the rigidity of a gaseous column"..."with such low frequencies as, say 10,000 per second which I was able to obtain without difficulty from a specially constructed alternator." "...how must a gaseous medium behave under the influence of enormous electrostatic stresses which may be active in the interstellar space, and which may alternate with inconceivable rapidity?"

In this respect, Tesla seemed also to address the omnidirectional ZPR. His statements also show he was attempting to make up his mind as to the characteristics of the ether, such as whether it is rigid or fluidic, and under what circumstances it may change, and its static or dynamic nature, of high or low density, and so fourth: "What determines the rigidity of a body? It must be the speed and amount of moving matter. In a gas the speed may be considerable, but the density is exceedingly small, in a liquid the speed would be likely to be small, though the density may be considerable; and in both cases, the inertia resistance asserts itself. A body might move with more or less freedom through the vibrating mass, but as a whole it would be rigid."

This statement reflects Tesla's prior tests, since, prior to his 1892 lectures in London, he had performed tests between two electrified plates, stating that the "space" between became "solid state" when subjected to "sufficiently high voltages and frequencies". This addressed the issue of how "solid bodies" can pass through a dense, vibrating, interpenetrating mass of ether which, as a whole is *rigid*. This is the essence of how the "inertia resistance" of the underlying 'ether framework' can be summoned up by an electrified body which activates the ether with currents of "sufficiently high voltage and frequency". As the inertial resistance of the ether "asserts itself", the electrified body is propelled through the ether by MHD thrust, which is really the "microhelical drills" at work.

63

The "specially constructed alternator" of which Tesla spoke was a 32-inch diameter one, which if similar to the type used on the saucer I saw in 1953, was probably driven by one of Tesla's bladeless turbines. In the 1890's, Tesla said the alternator had produced up to 10 amps and 30 kilocycles. One of these alternators is shown below:

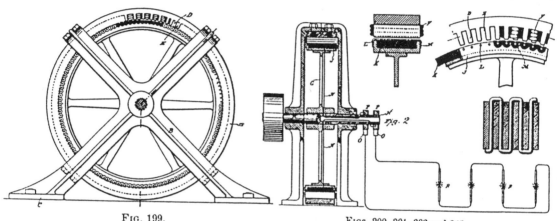

FIG. 199.   FIGS. 200, 201, 202 and 203.

The saucer I saw in 1953 exhibited precessional characteristics which could have been caused by the use of such an alternator, the output and rpms of which under the circumstances could have been varied with the power level of the saucer, as if it were being turned progressively faster by a turbine as the ship used more power to accelerate. The high angle and low frequency of the precessions would be consistent with the use of a high frequency, large diameter alternator, which was turned more slowly at hovering power, and increased in rpm for more power as the ship accelerated.

Since the alternator would likely have been attached ridigly to the airframe of the saucer, it could have caused the entire saucer to precess at hovering power, while the downward acceleration due to gravity was being balanced by the upward electropulsive acceleration, as the ship hovered in place above the earth. This phenomenon showed that the precession I observed in 1953 was either due to rotating internal machinery, or to the "virtual" angular momentum created by the electropulsive effects.

The balanced forces holding the ship in mid-air would have been equivalent to holding it on "gimbals of air", so that it precessed freely

64

according to the speed of the rotating alternator's angular momentum and mass. This would have required very little force, because the electropulsive forces reduced the ships inertia to almost zero. On the other hand, the rotatory force which a magnetic field imparts to electrical current, to create the microhelices, could be the cause of precession, as an "equal and opposite reaction", by collective rotatory precessive action imparted to all the atoms of the entire mass of the ship.

Tesla worked out the problem of how to counteract the tendency of the ship to rotate due to the torque of the alternator or turbine, by using two turbines or alternators, turned on parallel axes in the same direction or counter-rotated, as stated in his patent #1,655,114, *Apparatus for Aerial Transportation*, Jan. 3, 1928. In fact, a single alternator and turbine turning on separate , parallel axes, linked by a gear box, would accomplish the same thing.

As the ship accelerated to full speed and power, its low precessional rate and high precessional angle became a mere high-frequency wobble, as the ship shot to infinity in three seconds (which I estimated roughly 7.5 miles). This was consistent with the alternator being turned at a progressively higher speed. The rapid precessive wobble of the ship's periphery tended to blur its outline, something which has made it more difficult to obtain sharp definitions of the profiles of saucers in photographs and video. Coupled with this physical vibration may be the "Faraday effect"---the "magneto-optical effect" which tends to blur the outlines of objects subjected to intense electromagnetic fields. The extension of the ship's electric field also extends its magnetic field, and causes a rotation of the optical plane, so in addition to visual effects of the high frequency precessional oscillations, the optical plane is actually rotated to create the weird magneto-optical effects so often reported, and becomes distorted in the minds of the mystics, who think it is some sort of "time travel" or "interdimensional travel" effect, a "space-warpage" or "wrapping around" of "time and space" by a "rotating body" as it moves through space, *ala* Einstein, except saucers don't "revolve", as proven by my Peiltochterkompass, and Einstein was full of baloney.

The flying saucer may be powered by a Tesla alternator, a Tesla coil, or a combination of the two. Tesla stated that the required currents could be conveyed by conductor, which allows for the instantaneous control of a ship by means of high voltage stepping switches or relays. Since an on-board power generator is usually required anyway, the use of an alternator is more convenient than a spark gap, coil, and condenser combination, since the necessary high frequency alternations can be easily stepped up to higher voltages by several closely linked "extra" coils, placed about the ship.

It is possible that a ball-shaped cockpit was used on some of the German *Kreisel Tellers* ("Gyrating Saucers") of the 1940's. The ball-shaped cockpit would have been pressurized, mounted on gimbals, and gyro-stabilized with a horizontally oriented *Meisterkreiselkompass* ("Master-gyro-compass"), which would not only gyro-stabilize the cockpit while the outer saucer precessed wildly, but would provide the polar compass heading for the slave compass:

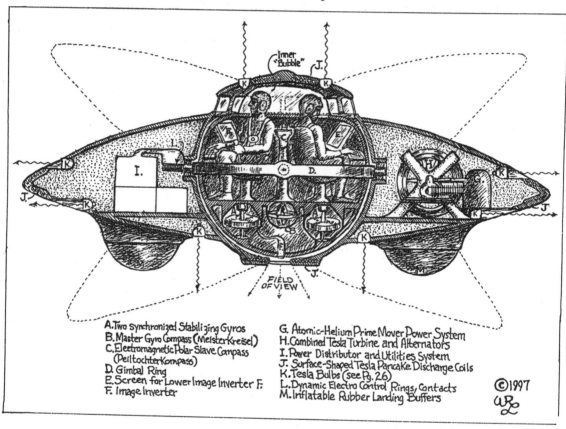

A. Two synchronized Stabilizing Gyros
B. Master Gyro Compass (MeisterKreisel)
C. Electromagnetic Polar Slave Compass (Peiltochter Kompass)
D. Gimbal Ring
E. Screen for Lower Image Inverter F.
F. Image Inverter
G. Atomic-Helium Prime Mover Power System
H. Combined Tesla Turbine and Alternators
I. Power Distributor and Utilities System
J. Surface-Shaped Tesla Pancake Discharge Coils
K. Tesla Bulbs (see Pg. 26)
L. Dynamic Electro Control Rings, Contacts
M. Inflatable Rubber Landing Buffers

©1997

As the outer ship precessed because the alternator was bolted to the outer airframe---the inner cockpit would be gyro-stabilized, so the pilot and crew could have visibility of the outer environment. Even with a precessional angle of 45 degrees, the pilot would still be able to see where he was, and where he was going. I could not see the top of the saucer I saw in 1953, so can't say what the visibility system was.

TESLA'S DYNAMIC THEORY OF GRAVITY

According to Tesla's lecture prepared for the Institute of Immigrant Welfare (May. 12, 1938), his *Dynamic Theory of Gravity* was one of two far reaching discoveries, which he "...worked out in all details", in the years 1893 and 1894. The 1938 lecture was less than five years before his death.

More complete statements concerning these discoveries can only be gleaned from scattered and sparse sources, because the papers of Tesla are concealed in government vaults for "national security" reasons. When I specifically asked for these papers at the "National Security Research Center"---now the "Robert J. Oppenheimer Research Center"---in 1979, I was denied access because they were classified, even though on that same day I discovered the plans for the hydrogen bomb on an open shelf, and told a Harvard graduate student about it later in the day at a Santa Fe restaurant. The guy went to Los Alamos, copied the plans, and wrote an expose at Harvard.

In his 1938 lecture, Tesla said he was progressing with the work, and hoped to give the theory to the world "very soon", so it was clearly his intent to "give it to the world", as soon as he had completed his secret developments.

The "two great discoveries" to which Tesla referred, were:

1. The Dynamic Theory of Gravity - which assumed a *field of force* which accounts for the motions of bodies in space; assumption of this field of force dispenses with the concept of *space curvature* (*ala* Einstein); the ether has an indispensable function in the phenomena (of universal gravity, inertia, momentum, and movement of heavenly bodies, as well as all atomic and molecular matter); and,

2. Environmental Energy - the Discovery of a new physical Truth: there is no energy in matter other than that received from the environment.

The usual Tesla birthday announcement---on his 79th birthday (1935)---Tesla made a brief reference to the theory saying it applies to molecules and atoms as well as to the largest heavenly bodies, and to "...all matter in the universe in any phase of its existence from its very formation to its ultimate disintegration".

Those imbued with relativist theory often refer to "pure energy" in some "form", but there is no such thing, since "energy" is an abstract "ability" which is always in the future. Who's to say what "form" is "pure", and what form is not?

My favorite philosopher, Ayn Rand, said. "In reality, there are no contradictions. Things are what they are irrespective as to whether we know it or not. Check your premises." If the term "energy" is only a convenient abstraction, then it does not exist in physical form, and really describes the potential to perform work as a by-product of matter and electromagnetic radiation in perpetual motion, some of the force of which has been diverted through a path where it performs the desired work, as it goes on its merry way through the universe. Every change of form of either matter or radiation involves the "work" which induces the change, or the "work" which is induced *by* the change. Without work there is *no* change, but all work is ultimately the product of the universe in perpetual, self-sustaining motion, as a rule and not an exception.

As for Tesla's theory, we have hints, such as, that the earth is the "star of human birth". In poetic expressions, he hid scientific meanings in statements such as, that using the "thunderbolt of Jove" (the Indo-European sky god), man "annihilates time and space", an allusion to the use of electro-propulsion ("thunderbolts"), to travel so fast, that time and space are "annihilated". Where the government has stolen his papers, we must search for meaning elsewhere. In an article, *Man's Greatest Achievement[1]*, Tesla outlined his *Dynamic Theory of Gravity* in poetic form (as paraphrased by me):

- That the luminiferous ether fills all space

- That the ether is acted upon by the life-giving creative force

- That the ether is thrown into "infinitesimal whirls" ("micro helices") at near the speed of light, becoming ponderable matter

- That when the force subsides and motion ceases, matter reverts to the ether (a form of "atomic decay")

---

[1]

John J. O'Neill, *Prodigal Genius*, 1944, pp. 251-252

▶   That man can harness these processes, to:
    -Precipitate matter from the ether
    -Create whatever he wants with the matter and energy
     derived
    -Alter the earth's size
    -Control earth's seasons (weather control)
    -Guide earth's path through the Universe, like a space
     ship
    -Cause the collisions of planets to produce new suns and
     stars, heat, and light
    -Originate and develop life in infinite forms

Tesla was referring to unlimited energy, derived from the environment. Several of his major free energy discoveries have been the exclusive stolen property of our Secret Government. The conversion of energy to a stronger force---electropulsion---used to control the much weaker gravity force, would accomplish more work in the same amount of time, and produce "over unity" results.

Some of Telsa's unusual conceptualization of the ether had been nonetheless expounded piecemeal, in his preceding 1890's lectures.[2] He later railed against the limited and erroneous theories of Maxwell, Hertz, Lorentz, and Einstein.

Tesla's ether was neither the "solid" ether with the "tenuity of steel" of Maxwell and Hertz, nor the half-hearted, entrained, gaseous ether of Lorentz. Tesla's ether consisted of "carriers immersed in an insulating fluid", which filled all space. Its properties varied according to relative movement, the presence of mass, and the electric and magnetic environment.

Tesla's ether was rigidified by rapidly varying electrostatic forces, and was thereby involved in gravitational effects, inertia, and momentum, especially in the space near earth, since, as explained by Tesla, the earth is "...like a charged metal ball moving through space", which creates the enormous, rapidly varying electrostatic forces which diminish in intensity with the square of the distance from earth, just like gravity. Since the direction of propagation radiates from the earth, the

---

[2] T. C. Martin, *Inventions, Researches and Writings of Nicola Tesla*, 1894, Chapter XXV - *Introduction - The Scope of the Tesla Lectures.*

so-called force of gravity is toward earth.

Tesla commenced to complete his *Dynamic Theory of Gravity* at the same approximate period of time that his experimental results and theories had been revealed in the three lectures, often illustrated with demonstrations using Tesla-invented equipment, as revealed in the following eight excerpts, in pertinent part (emphasis mine):

1. "The most probable medium filling the space is one consisting of *independent carriers immersed in an insulating fluid*".

2. "In his experiments he dwells first on some phenomena produced by *electrostatic force, which he considers in the light of modern theories to be the most important force in nature for us to investigate.*"

3. "*He illustrates how mechanical motions are produced by a varying electrostatic force acting through a gaseous medium.*"

4. "One of the *most interesting results* arrived at in pursuing these experiments, is *the demonstration of the fact that a gaseous medium upon which vibration is impressed by rapid changes of electrostatic potential, is rigid.*"

5. "If through this medium enormous electrostatic stresses are assumed to act, which vary rapidly in intensity, it would allow the motion of a body through it, yet it would be rigid and elastic, although the fluid itself might be devoid of these properties".

6. "...on the assumption that the independent carriers are of any configuration such that the fluid resistance to motion in one direction is greater than in another, a stress of that nature would cause the carriers to arrange themselves in groups, since they would *turn to each other their sides of the greatest electrical density*, in which position the *fluid resistance to approach would be smaller than to receding.*"

7. "If in a medium of the above characteristics a brush would be formed by a steady potential, an exchange of the carriers would go on continuously, and there would be less carriers per unit volume in the brush than in the space at some distance from the electrode, this corresponding to rarefaction".

8. "If the potentials were rapidly changing, the result would be very different; the higher the frequency of the pulses, the slower would be the exchange of carriers; finally, the motion of translation through measurable space would cease and, with a sufficiently high frequency and intensity of the stress, the carriers would be drawn towards the electrode, and compression would result."

The eight above excerpts are further reducible to the following four statements pertinent to electro-propulsion technology:

1. Mechanical motions can be produced by varying electrostatic force acting through a gaseous (ether) medium, which thereby becomes rigidified, yet allows solid bodies to pass through.

2. Under influence of stress in one direction (under the polarizing influence of light or heat), the carriers may group together, forming tubes of force, creating greater ease of movement in that direction.

3. When a (D.C.) brush is created by a steady potential, a continuous exchange of carriers is created corresponding to ether rarefaction, as the tubes of force are drawn into the conductor.

4. With a sufficiently high frequency and stress intensity in the opposite direction, carrier exchange is blocked by ether compression, forcing the tubes of force to dissolve in the conductors of the ship, imparting electromagnetic momentum. The system, using the two kinds of potentials (D.C. and A.C.), is known as "p2".

The steady potential of the brush creates the required exchange of carriers, 'rarifying' (stretching) the elastic, rigidified medium (composed of the carriers immersed in the insulating fluid) in advance of the ship, as the high frequency A.C. to the rear compresses them, blocking exchange from the rear, dissolving the tubes of force (my "microhelices"), creating instant momentum, normal to the surface (which is at right angles to the electric and magnetic fields).

In 1884, John Henry Poynting's theorem had been that the flux of energy at any place is represented by the vector product of the electric and magnetic forces, multiplied by $C/4\pi$.[3] This implied that forces in a conductor could be transformed there into other forms. In 1893, J. J. Thomson stated practically the same thing, saying "...the aether is itself the vehicle of mechanical momentum, of amount $(1/4\pi C)$ $(D \cdot B)$ per unit volume.[4]

(Using e.-s. Units for D and E
and e.-m. Units for B and H.)

---

[3] *Phil. Trans.* clxxv (1884), p. 343.

[4] *Recent Researches in Elect. and Mag.* (1893), p. 13.

E = electrical force
D = electrical displacement
H = magnetic force
B = magnetic induction

Heinrich Hertz's theory[5] was that two systems of varying current should exert a ponderomotive force on each other due to the variations. Tesla's disagreement was apparently based on the fact that he proved that the "ponderomotive force" is due not to mere "varying currents", but to rarefaction and compression of the ether carriers, respectively, produced by *different kinds of currents* (D.C., A.C., rapidly varying electrostatic).

J. J. Thomson[6] had extensively developed the theory of the moving tubes of force, both magnetic and electric, saying that the magnetic effect was a secondary one created by the movement of electric tubes, and assumed:

▸ that tubes exist everywhere in space, either in closed circuits or terminating on atoms;

▸ that electric force becomes perceivable only when electric tubes have greater tendency to lie in one direction;

▸ that in a steady magnetic field, positive and negative tubes may move in opposite directions with equal velocity;

▸ that a beam of light is a group of electric tubes moving at C at right angles to their length (providing a good explanation for polarization of the plane of rotation).

Tesla said his "dirigible torpedo" would fly at a maximum 300 miles per second, perhaps since its forward velocity would be some maximum fraction of C. Thomson's later publishings on this subject followed Tesla's 1891 lectures before the Royal Society in London, and appear to shed light on Tesla's work, stating:

▸ that a ponderomotive force is exerted on a conductor carrying electric current, consisting of a transfer of mechanical momentum from the agent which exerts the force to the body which

---

[5] *Ann. d. Phys.* Xxxi (1887), p. 421; *Hertz's Electric Waves*, translated by D.E. Jones, p. 29.

[6] *Recent Researches in Elect. And Mag.* (1893), p. 13.

72

experiences it;

- ► that, if moving tubes entering a conductor are dissolved in it, mechanical momentum is given to the conductor;
- ► that such momentum must be at right angles to the tube and to the magnetic induction;
- ► that momentum stored in a unit volume of the field is proportional to the vector product of electric and magnetic vectors.

"Thomson's" *Electromagnetic Momentum* hypothesis was later developed by H. Poincaré[7] and by M. Abraham[8].

By 1910, it was said[9] that the consequence of these pronouncements left three alternatives:

1. Modify the theory to reduce to zero the resultant force on an element of free aether (as with Maxwell, Hertz, and Einstein);

2. Assume the force sets aether in motion (as with Helmholtz);

3. Accept the principle that aether is the vehicle of mechanical momentum of amount $[D \cdot B]$ per unit volume (as with Poynting and J. J. Thomson).

Whittaker's greatest error was in omitting Tesla's theory entirely. After Tesla's experiments verified it, right in front of the esteemed members of the "Royal Academy", the "three (later) alternatives" were moot, and a new law existed, that of Tesla.

Tesla's Secrecy

Due to his pacifist sympathies, Tesla originally contemplated giving his electric flying machine to the Geneva Convention or League of Nations, for use in 'policing the world' to prevent war. Later disillusioned after WWI with the collapse of the League, he said he'd "...underestimated man's combative capacity".[10]

---

[7] *Archives Né erl.* (2) v (1900), p. 252.

[8] *Gött., Nach.*, 1902, p. 20.

[9] Sir Edmund Whittaker, *A History of the Theories of the Aether and Electricity*, 1910, Edinborough.

[10] *New York Times*, July 10, 1934.

In 1919, his reason for increased secrecy emerged in an interview with Frederick M. Kerby, for *Resolution* magazine, while discussing a "three-hour" airplane between New York and London: "...we have here the appalling prospect of a war between nations at a distance of thousands of miles, with weapons so destructive and demoralizing that the world could not endure them. That is why there must be no more war." With the government's spurning of his defense suggestions, Tesla's only recourse was to withhold his secrets from the world, and to dissuade discovery in their direction.

In 1929, Tesla ridiculed Heinrich Hertz's 1887-89 experiments purportedly proving the Maxwellian "structureless" ether filling all space, "of inconceivable tenuity yet solid and possessed of rigidity incomparably greater than the hardest steel". Tesla's arguments were to the contrary, saying he had always believed in a "gaseous" ether in which he had observed waves more akin to sound waves. He recounted how he had developed a "new form of vacuum tube" in 1896 (which I call the "Tesla bulb"), "...capable of being charged to any desired potential, and operated it with effective pressures of about 4,000,000 volts." He described how purplish coronal discharges about the bulb when in use, verified the existence of "particles smaller than air", and a gas so light that an earth-sized volume would weigh only 1/20 pound. He further said sound waves moved at the velocity of light through this medium.[11]

Tesla mentioned using his special tube to investigate cosmic rays[12], saying that when its emanations were impinged upon a target material, radioactive emissions resulted, and that radioactive bodies were simply "targets" continuously bombarded by "infinitesimal bullets projected from all parts of the universe", without which "all radioactivity would cease." His description of these "bullets" was similar to the ZPR.

On Apr. 15, 1932[13], Tesla said Einstein's theory regarding changing matter into force, and force into matter, was "absurd". He compared this to the difference between body and mind, saying force is a

---

[11] *New York Herald Tribune*, Sept. 22, 1929, pp. 1, 29.

[12] Letter, *New York Times*, Feb. 6, 1932, p. 16, col. 8.

[13] *Nikola Tesla Papers*, Rare Books and Manuscript Library, Columbia University.

"...function of matter", and that, just as a mind could not exist without a body, "...without matter, there can be no force."

On Sept. 11, 1932 (*New York Herald Tribune*), Tesla derided the Maxwellian/Hertzian ether, while saying that higher frequency waves "...follow the curvature of the earth and bend around obstacles", yet in an Apr. 8, 1934 *New York Times* letter, said that short waves for "power purposes" of the 'wireless art', were inappropriate, and that power will travel in "long waves". His 1929 attack on the Maxwellian/Hertzian ether theory---39 years afterward, during the advent of Relativism---seemed relevant only to his concealed theory, not to disclose it or promote it, but to conceal it.

THE NATURE OF ELECTRICITY

What were the old ether physicists referring to when they attempted to describe "an incompressible, perfect fluid"? What would a "perfect fluid" do? It would be able to "wet" everything it came into contact with, such as protons, and could flow everywhere without resistance. One "fluid"---the ether---could flow everywhere, and because of its density and ultra-fineness, nothing could stop it, and it felt no resistance, but only matter felt resistance, depending on the circumstances. Another fluid---electricity---could flow in certain places, and wet only certain things, but often met resistance.

In order to understand the ether, we must get to know electricity more intimately. Just like water, a proton will hold only so much electricity on its surface, but the 'surface' of the proton is probably similar to the outer area of a ball-shaped swarm of hovering mechanical bees, powered by the ZPR, with a denser agglomeration of "bees" toward the 'ball's' center. If this swarm of bees is subjected to a wave of rainy mist (the etheric 'wind'), the bees must all turn to face into the etheric wind to maintain their formation. The 'water' droplets---electric sub-charges carried by the etheric wind---tend to agglomerate around the front side. Each bee, as he flaps his wings, will get wet only so much, so that excess 'water' is thrown off and carried to the next bee, or the next swarm of bees, by the etheric wind, and so forth, so that a 'current' of droplets continues to flow through the ball of bees due to its motion through the etheric wind, and transfers momentum between masses.

The 'water' tends to come off in larger drops, which have formed from smaller droplets accumulated on each bee. As in fluid mechanics, the 'drop' size is the result of cohesiveness of the electric 'fluid', the surface area of each 'bee', and the space between each bee, all of which influences the final size of each larger 'drop' (the "electron") which accumulates enough to form it. If one were to mathematically analyze the flow of "drops" (i.e., "quanta") per mass unit, they would have an average rate   of the flow of charges/cm^3, of etheric wind, for the momentum, as determined by the "current" flow rate.

Much like the bees, as a body (its many electrons, atoms, and molecules, with plenty of 'space' within and between) sits at rest on the earth, it moves at fantastic speed through the universal ether field, due to the earth's revolution, orbit, and other motions.

In his 1891 A.I.E.E. lecture at Columbia College, Tesla said in pertinent part (emphasis mine): "What is electricity, and what is magnetism? "...We are now confident that electric and magnetic phenomena are attributable to the ether, and we are perhaps justified in saying that the effects of static electricity are effects of ether in motion". "...we may speak of electricity or of an electric condition, state or effect". "...we must distinguish two such effects, opposite in character neutralizing each other". "...for in a medium of the properties of the ether, we cannot possibly exert a strain, or produce a displacement or motion of any kind, without causing in the surrounding medium an equivalent and opposite effect." "...its condition determines the positive and negative character." "We know that it acts like an incompressible fluid;" "...the electro-magnetic theory of light and all facts observed teach us that electric and ether phenomena are identical." "The puzzling behavior of the ether as a solid to waves of light and heat, and as a fluid to the motion of bodies through it, is certainly explained in the most natural and satisfactory manner by assuming it to be in motion, as Sir William Thomson has suggested." "Nor can anyone prove that there are transverse ether waves emitted from an alternate current machine; to such slow disturbances, the ether, if at rest, may behave as a true fluid."

In his statements, Tesla was balancing the various arguments in preparation for his decision: "...Electricity, therefore, cannot be called ether in the broad sense of the term; but nothing would seem to stand in the way of calling electricity ether associated with matter, or bound ether; or, in other words, that the so-called static charge of the molecule is ether associated in some way with the molecule."

"...It cannot differ in density, ether being incompressible: it must, therefore, be under some strain or in motion, and the latter is the most probable." Tesla therefore believed in an ether which was in motion relative to earth, because the earth is in motion.

The thing which Tesla had realized, was that ether possesses electric charges which are deposited on atoms. In supporting the "dynamic" ether concept, he was supporting the "stationary ether" concept, since the "motion" he referred to was "apparent" motion of the ether perceived by an observer on earth, relative to a stationary ether.

The importance of cosmic motion to the electromagnetic effects of static charges was brought up by Tesla in his lecture: "About fifteen years ago, Prof. Rowland demonstrated a most interesting and important fact, namely, that a static charge carried around produces the effects of an electric current." "...and conceiving the electrostatically charged molecules in motion, this experimental fact gives us a fair idea of magnetism. We can conceive lines or tubes of force which physically exist, being formed of rows of directed moving molecules; we can see that these lines must be closed, that they must tend to shorten and expand, etc. It likewise explains in a reasonable way, the most puzzling phenomenon of all, permanent magnetism, and, in general, has all the beauties of the Ampere theory without possessing the vital defect of the same, namely, the assumption of molecular currents. Without enlarging further upon the subject, I would say, that I look upon all electrostatic, current and magnetic phenomena as being due to electrostatic molecular forces."

In these statements, Tesla showed he was aware that any "stationary" locale on earth is actually in fantastic motion ("70,000 mph"). The electrostatic charges "carried around" are currents between atoms and the ether, which produce magnetism. The phenomena of 'permanent magnetism' or 'cosmically induced' magnetism are apparently due to electrostatic charges 'carried around' by cosmic motion, in the universal ether field.

Since no one can hold an atom or molecule perfectly still---because it is in fantastic motion---all atoms and molecules carry currents producing magnetic fields. Since a magnetic field is the product of a current, no one can produce a magnetic field without electricity, moving through or along a conductor, or as electrostatic charges in local or cosmic motion.

Tesla's *Dynamic Theory of Gravity* and MHD method of Spacial Electropulsion brought a cosmic crowning achievement to the works of Faraday, Wm. Thomson, J. J. Thomson, and Edmund Hall.

CONCLUSION

The ether is a universal medium, which fills all space. It appears to be "dynamic" relative to an earth moving thousands of miles per hour through space. The ether is normally electrically neutral, ultra-fine, and penetrates all solid matter. There is also an ultra high frequency, ubiquitous radiation, normally in equilibrium, called Zero Point Radiation ("ZPR"), which interpenetrates the ether, and represents electromagnetic radiation in its finest, densest form, which, in conjunction with the ether, conserves universal perpetual motion.

The ether in conjunction with the ZPR, is the source of all matter and force. "Energy" does not exist in physical form, but is "the ability to do work", which is equal to "force over time". The word "energy" is a convenient fiction, like "time", which is an arbitrary measurement of the rate of motion of matter through ether-filled space. All events occur in the present, and the "past" and "future" are merely metaphors.

Electromagnetic disturbances in the ether extract "energy" from the ZPR, which is explainable only by an ether theory. This "free energy", which is virtually unlimited, is universally at work, created by the perpetual motion of matter, and the perpetual exchange of stronger and weaker forces, through which the equilibrium of the universe is maintained, the sum total of all processes equaling zero.

Since all solid matter is continually hurling through space, always in motion, it is always subjected to the "etheric wind" and ZPR interactions. These effects are not perceived except during changes in the orientation of mass or its velocity. All mass and space have dielectric properties. Differences in dielectric properties cause changes in the electromagnetic displacement within mass and the etheric wind. Earth's electric field creates dielectric displacement effects within ether and mass within earth's electric field. The difference between the dielectric displacement within a mass and the dielectric displacement outside the mass in the etheric wind, creates a down-force in the direction of the negative polarity, as the etheric wind 'blows' through a mass. This is called "gravity".

Since all mass is in motion, all mass has momentum, even when apparently "at rest" relative to earth. Momentum is a body's resistance to change in its state of motion. Since inertia is also the resistance of a body to changes in its momentum, inertia and momentum are due to the same thing, the resistance of electromagnetic micro helical tubules to changes in velocity (and relative "pitch"), direction, and lateral motions or orientation. Since all space and mass is composed only of "electric content", momentum/inertia is electromagnetic in nature, and can be electromagnetically synthesized.

All mass contains electrostatic charges, which when "carried around" in the ether/ZPR-filled space by celestial or 'local' movement, constitute currents. These currents actually flow between mass and the ether, and are integral to the mechanism by which momentum is imparted to mass in motion. The currents create magnetic fields as their equal-and-opposite counterparts, and give a rotatory motion to combined, bi-directional electric and magnetic fields and currents, around irrotational vacuous ether cores. This rotatory electromagnetic action creates momentum, as the force-free "screw-type" reaction within mass, creating its motion relative to the ether cores, from which the mechanical force is transferred to the atomic mass with which the electromagnetism is associated.

Since these phenomena are electromagnetic in nature, they are synthesized by recreation of the electromagnetic conditions which a body would exhibit due to a particular kinetic state. Just as electromagnetic waves of low frequency can penetrate a body, waves of higher frequencies---above I.R. and below U.V.---can cause the ether to "assert its inertia resistance".

The technology involves high voltage D.C. 'brush' currents, high frequency currents, rapidly varying electrostatic forces, and light/heat beams. The rapidly varying electrostatic forces "rarify" (stretch) the ether carriers, as the light/heat beams polarize the medium in the desired direction, as the D.C. brush currents induce the exchange of carriers, creating a vacuum in that direction, inducing motion. At the opposite end of the ship, high frequency currents draw the carriers through the ship, and creates a compression of the ether, as it penetrates the solid mass and synthesizes the rotatory micro helical tubules, which whirl around the ether cores along the polar axis, at a pitch corresponding to a particular rate of momentum. Since the strength of the electromagnetic interaction is 10^{40} time greater than the gravitational interaction, that much more work can theoretically be done in the same time, using the same "energy".

Since "seeing is believing", and I have seen, I believe. The behavior of man-made flying saucers proves the existence of these "free energy" inventions of Nikola Tesla, which show that he was right in his opposition to Relativism, and that the prevalent theories taught in the scientific institutions of the world are patently <u>fraudulent.</u>

Consistent with the idea that "dynamite comes in small packages", this small book, along with my prior book, *Space Aliens From the Pentagon*, initiates the rediscovery, reconstruction and publication of Nikola Tesla's *Dynamic Theory of Gravity* and related *electropulsion* technology, the greatest invention of mankind.

The Secret Government---a fraudulently concealed, unconstitutional, corporate-state entity---has heretofore controlled electropulsion technology by concealing it and other advanced free energy technology, on behalf of international, coercive, corporate-state monopolists. Electropulsive ships are concealed through "special effects", and "stealth technology" (also based on Nikola Tesla's inventions)---as they fly and hover in the sky, and by "psycho-political" means---the dissemination of false "alien" and "extraterrestrial origin" propaganda---through "UFOlogy" groups led by covert government agents. While official government spokesmen deny the existence of flying saucers, covert government agents, posing as "skeptics", "UFOlogists", and "paranormalists", engage the public's attention in a phony debate. The "skeptics" ridicule the UFOlogists and paranormalists, lumping them together with rational witnesses, as if "...to see a flying saucer" is as ridiculous as "...to see a ghost or alien". This phony debate based on false logic fits nicely into the overall cover-up system, designed to conceal "advanced <u>human</u> technology", not "alien" technology.

The grip of this secret socio-economic dictatorship, depends on coercively extorted income, by forcing us to buy archaic fuel and power---which funds their control of our communications, political and monetary decisions, enforcement of unjust laws, regulations, and procedures expanding its powers, while limiting or excluding our individual human rights, and denying our access to information, materials, and technology which is <u>ours</u> because we paid for it with our taxes. Our access to the truth is necessary for our independence and survival as a free people.

Despite the confusion, concealment, BIG LIES, and judicial and socio-economic abuse by the corporate state, we can resurrect the TRUTH, determine the correct technology, circumvent obstructions, and use our creative ingenuity to build these ships for ourselves, to free our society from the Secret Fascist Corpocracy.

Chapter VI: FREE ENERGY MASSACRE;
The Atomic Hydrogen Process
©1996, WM. R. LYNE

What better way to end a book on "Occult Ether Physics", than with a chapter on another concealed "free energy" process, which appears to extract energy from the ether---using similar techniques on the same substance that makes Tesla's electro-propulsion possible?

In *SPACE ALIENS*, I specified a free energy process in which helium is made to produce 460,000 calories/gram-atom, by simple spark discharge, which is based on data from numerous generally available texts and scientific encyclopedias. This is the highest energy output I know of from a noble gas, and the same gas can be used *ad infinitum*, the only input energy being that required for spark discharges. Since helium is inappropriate for the average "Joe", and since the output is probably more than you could handle, I will more appropriately show you how to perform another free energy process, using that most easily accessible gas, hydrogen. I will also give you the explanation for the heat produced in so-called "cold fusion", and a few other free energy processes, all closely related to the atomic hydrogen process and occult ether physics.

Over the years, the "Relativistic Quantum Mechanics" (hence, "RQMs") concealed every process or reaction which could show the invalidity of their theories, "...in the interest of national security". Their false theories actually became one of the most important means by which, from the standpoint of the government's secret agencies, that "national secrets" were concealed, while at the same time, from the standpoint of the controlling corporate fascists, all 'dangerously efficient' technology which would destroy their iron grip on us, could be concealed. According to deceitful relativist quantum mechanics, all energy coming out of a reaction, must go into the reaction, only from a "non-ether" source recognized by them, *and only in the discrete "quanta" permitted by their misapplication of Max Planck's earlier quantum theory.* The basic idea of Planck's original quantum mechanical theory, was that energy levels of atoms must change in whole number integers (1,2,3, etc.), called "quanta", which are based on the basic charge of a single electron, which assumes only certain assigned energy levels in different atoms and molecules, and is used to define the magnitude of all of the smallest, intermediate, and largest possible energy changes of atoms and molecules. All atomic energy changes must conform to the permissible whole number equivalents or multiples of these quanta. Accordingly, energy absorbed by an atom must fit this stringent criterion. Despite what I consider to be obvious attempts to conceal basic physical data conflicting with this principle---as misinterpreted by the Relativists and incorporated into their theory, as if it were exclusively their theory and not that published earlier by Planck---the process I am about to discuss with you has glaring inconsistencies in it, even as described and *mis*-measured by the Relativists. It is said by them that the process of dissociating diatomic hydrogen molecules into separate atoms as atomic hydrogen, requires the absorption of 109,000 cal./gram molecule ("1.9 k.cal./gram molecule"). Yet, in taking the basic hydrogen atom and considering all its discrete 'quanta'---whether in the atomic or molecular state---it appears to me that there is no state of the hydrogen atom or molecule in which such energy could be "stored", even when using the RQMs' theories, especially in view of their irrational statement that the energy is still possessed by the molecule after it has already been released! It is their contention that an independent hydrogen atom can only exist as such because it has absorbed an abnormally large amount of heat, despite the fact that by their own criteria the atom has no mechanism identifiable by them by which it could do so. When two such hydrogen atoms come together with the presence of sufficient initiation energy, the great amount of heat said by the Relativists to be stored in the hydrogen atom is liberated. The RQMs never directly measured the amount of dissociation energy necessary to bring the hydrogen atom from the diatomic to the atomic state, because they didn't know how to do so, but because their theory said that "all reactions are reversible", they said the dissociation energy was the same as the energy released on recombination of hydrogen atoms. Then to make matters worse, they defined the atomic hydrogen (ground) state as if it were an excited state, and the molecular state as if it were the ground state.

Realistically, the atomic hydrogen reaction can only be satisfactorily explained by reference to, construction of, or re-construction of, an ether theory. While it may be arguable that the "binding energy" between the two atoms of the molecule somehow 'includes' this energy in some undefined and mysterious way, this argument actually supports an ether theory, because the binding energy must somehow be exchanged with the energy which is released when the molecule forms, consistent with the equal and opposite reaction rule. Otherwise, one is

82

expected to believe a kind of backwards Orwellian *doublethink* kind of thing that the RQMs have perpetrated, since "...everything is like *relative*, man." This kind of latitude is permitted only for them, while those who disagree are held to a higher standard.

The doublethink features of Relativism stem from the fact that Albert Einstein was a Kaballist-Existentialist---and an *Illuminist*---whose epistemology was a *Platonist* one. In philosophy, there are two basic epistemologies---theories of the origin, nature and limits of human knowledge---representing the two basic categories into which the epistemologies of all philosophies must fall, and which are supposed to explain how one knows something according to a particular philosophy...by *what means* they know it...if in fact, they do "know" it. Since he who asserts something has the burden of proving it, rather than one who disbelieves it, the *means* by which it is purportedly known, may come into question. No one is legally, morally, or 'spiritually' obligated to believe anything, without reason, or a *valid means* of knowing it to be "true". All epistemologies are classified as either *Platonist*, or *Aristotelian*.

The "Platonist Epistemology" is so named because of the theory illustrated by the *cave analogy*, in the ancient Greek Philosopher, Plato's book, *The Republic*. In Plato's *cave analogy*, an observer inside a cave, facing the inner wall at night, sees only the shadows cast upon the wall by such things as a passing caravan, projected by a fire burning beyond a road along which a caravan is passing. According to Plato, man cannot *know* reality, but sees only a '*shadow*' of reality, because there is a 'higher world' of 'perfect forms', which exist only 'in heaven'. It therefore becomes obvious how this epistemology follows religious thinking, and that many religions have been influenced by it as somehow adding 'scientific credence' to their religious ideas, which are based on faith rather than reason. The same reasoning has been used by scientific, philosophical, economic, political, and 'spiritual' con-artists for centuries, and every totalitarian philosophy ever known has relied upon this fallacious 'reasoning' which is identical to the Platonist epistemology. One wonders how the viewer in Plato's cave would draw the line between 'knowing' a shadow, and a "shadow of a shadow", since a shadow might also have a 'higher form', under this theory.

The "Aristotelian Epistemology" in the meanwhile---based on the ancient Greek philosopher Aristotle's theory---holds that the senses are valid, scientific tools of cognition, which we can rely upon, to detect the facts of perceivable reality, and that we can, by relying upon the facts so perceived, know reality and determine other, perhaps unperceivable facts of reality.

As can be seen from a comparison of these two epistemologies and their implications, the philosophies and endeavors based on the Platonist Epistemology are mystical flaky, and/or <u>totalitarian,</u> while the philosophies and endeavors relying on the Aristotelian Epistemology are more rational and objective, especially when applied to the natural sciences. It can also be seen that the use of a Platonist Epistemology by a physicist should be considered unforgivable, while Einstein's theory, built upon this fatally flawed epistemology, has been popularized by the communication monopoly controlled by the power-elite, because it makes a potentially inquisitive and questioning society dumber and easier to control. Einstein's image is continually built up as if that of an ultimate and infallible creature who should be regarded as a 'god'. This propaganda not only protects the false theory, but also aids in concealment of valid theory and advanced technology which would end the reign of a world-wide power structure of corporate-statists, who think society already has all the technology it 'needs', else the elite's 'grip' on the world, held in place by their archaic technology which exploits mineral, industrial, and banking interests owned by them, might be torn loose.

I would have very little quarrel with a quantum theory of atomic energy levels, were it extended to include an ether theory, as it *should* have been logically construed, but I take issue with its present development, limitation, and misapplication by the RQMs. My position is that they *already have* applied it to an ether theory, that this application is well concealed, and that this book is needed to begin the reconstruction of these concealed truths, for use by the public. While Planck said his quantum theory applied to a "system", he didn't say the Relativist's "system"---which came into existence after his theory---was the only system it could be applied to. Since a rationally extended quantum mechanical theory would not exclude an ether, my "RQM" label distinguishes between the relativistic misinterpreters of quantum mechanics, and what could be called the "Integrated Reality Mechanics" ("IRMs").

The atomic hydrogen reaction first came to my attention in 1964, when I was studying industrial processes at Sam Houston State University, in Huntsville, Texas, the year after taking an introductory

84

course in college physics. While reviewing various welding processes in a textbook, my eyes fixed on an older process called "atomic hydrogen welding". By that time, the process was already considered "obsolete". To me, the process seemed valuable, not only because it produces such high temperatures---above 3400° F.---enough to melt tungsten---the highest temperatures producible by man---but is also "self-shielding", and can be used to weld diverse metals, often without flux, with a concentrated flame producing little heat distortion, when welding thin metal. In the process, 'normal' diatomic H_2 is shot through an electric arc which dissociates it into "atomic" hydrogen, H_1. This atomic hydrogen recombines at the (welded) metal surface, producing the very high heat. Though the process interested me then, and always has, I have never seen an atomic hydrogen welding unit for sale, for the 31 years hence. Industry's obvious excuse for laying the valuable process aside was that it had been 'replaced' by 'better' processes, such as *Heliarc*, TIG, and MIG welding, though they rarely mention "plasma arc welding", which has also almost disappeared from the market. Since plasma arc welding is merely an extension of the atomic hydrogen process, using a specially redesigned torch, the 'mysterious' reasons are undoubtedly the same.

The process simmered in the inner recesses of my mind for a few years until 1976, when I rekindled my interest in the process for possible use in welding stainless steel and reducing and fusing platinum metal compounds, because hydrogen reduces such compounds (which must also be shielded from oxygen) to metals. The atomic hydrogen process does not rely upon the combustion of hydrogen with oxygen in the air, but upon the "atomic" energy released when atomic hydrogen recombines to form the 'normal', diatomic hydrogen. I still had some unanswered questions, since the various welding data at my disposal failed to mention sufficient specific details. If Nikola Tesla was right, then I am right, that the energy comes from the ether.

Because I knew of no source from which to purchase an atomic hydrogen torch, I decided to build one, but my information was inadequate for proper construction. In the torch I made, the hydrogen gas entered the arc concentrically, around both electrodes, instead of passing through the arc at a right angle. I also used the wrong kind of arc transformer, so it didn't work as well as it should have.

Despite the disappointment, I knew the torch would work better if I corrected the problems, so I kept the torch in my barn until better information and sufficient time was available. I excited the curiosity of the industrial spooks, when I rented a large tank of hydrogen at a local welder's supply, and this probably contributed to the sudden acceleration of the CIA-maintained judicial harassment I endured between 1974 and 1992 (18 years). They apparently assumed I was exploring the process for its energy potential, rather than for just welding, and they were correct. My torch is shown below:

In the '70s, I had acquired an old English inorganic chemistry textbook[1], purchased from Los Alamos Scientific Laboratory salvage for $.25, which contained a halftone photo of a '30s-vintage atomic hydrogen welding torch, along with some basic data. The torch shown was different from the one I constructed, in that it used a high voltage arc transformer, and had no mechanism to strike the arc electrodes together to start the arc, because the high voltage made it unnecessary. It also showed the gas passing at right angle through the arc. In this old textbook, it was stated at page 170 (emphasis mine), as follows: *"Langmuir (1912) discovered that hydrogen at low pressure in contact with a tungsten wire heated by an electric current is dissociated to some extent into atoms:"...."This* <u>*absorbs*</u> *a large amount of energy, about 100 kcal. Per gram-molecule." "...The atomic hydrogen formed is chemically very active. Atomic hydrogen is formed when an electric arc between tungsten electrodes is allowed to burn in hydrogen at atmospheric pressures (Fig. 106)".*

The text continued:

"Atomic-hydrogen blown out of the arc by a jet of molecular hydrogen across the arc, forms an intensely hot flame, capable of melting tungsten (m. Pt. 3400°). This flame obtains its heat from recombination of hydrogen atoms to H_2."

"Hydrogen being set free in a chemical reaction is often more reactive than hydrogen gas."

"...the activity of such <u>nascent</u> (newborn) hydrogen, in the act of liberation from its compounds, is due to the hydrogen being in the <u>atomic state</u>."

The following is a copy of "fig. 106":

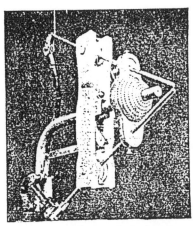

Fig. 106.—The atomic hydrogen blowpipe.

In checking this data in a more recent Van Nostrand's Encyclopedia of Science[2], at page 1311 it was stated in pertinent part:

"Hydrogen molecules dissociate to atoms endothermically at high temperatures (heat of dissociation about 103 cal/gram mole) in an electric arc, or by irradiation." "...the hydrogen atoms recombine at the metal surface to provide heat required for welding."

I was surprised to find this in the Van Nostrand encyclopedia, but I also found that in 1910, the D. Van Nostrand Company published a book by Haller and Cunningham, entitled *The High Frequency Coil*, (The construction of a Tesla Coil for the advanced amateur. 119 pages), so there is a record of sorts, of Van Nostrand's association with Tesla.

SMOKESCREENS FROM ACADEMIA

It seemed odd to me that it was later suggested that the 103 calories of dissociation energy absorbed from a very brief exposure to the arc is the same heat as that "...required for welding" as described, and I believed it to be more reasonable that the excess heat had to come from "elsewhere". The dissociation energy would be analogical to a <u>slice</u> of bread (@4 cal. gram), and the gross output would be equivalent to <u>60 loaves</u> of bread (@1814 cal. lb.), calorie-wise. There was too much disparity between the two, with plenty of suspicious omissions and confusions, in an obvious attempt to cover up the truth in between.

The older text showed the clearer construction of a device, and the newer text showed that only 103 cal./gram mole were required for dissociation, while the older text showed that 100,000 cal./gram mole were liberated on recombination. Only by jumping back and forth between the two sources was I able to put a complete documentation together, and discover the conflicts.

It was apparent from the newer text, that the writers intended for us to believe that the final 100 k.cal./gram molecule heat---later upped to 109 k.cal/gram molecule---was absorbed from the arc, but the 103 cal./gram molecule dissociation heat figure showed a net 108,897 cal./gram molecule unexplained. If there are about 65 cubic centimeters per mole of hydrogen at its critical volume, it seemed highly unlikely that sufficient energy to weld could be absorbed from the 'dissociating arc', during the time required for 65 cubic centimeters of gas to pass from the orifice and through the arc.

109,000 cal./gram mole equals 432.6 BTU/gram mole--- roughly the heat energy contained in <u>60 loaves of bread</u>---the "extra heat energy" which they have asked us to believe is 'stored' in an amount of atomic hydrogen which weighs 1/28th of an ounce, during its brief passage through the arc! How could the transformer produce that much energy, especially when it uses only half what it does in conventional welding processes? It seems more likely that excess heat could be stored in molecules than in 'almost naked' atomic hydrogen atoms. What ever happened to Bohr's little atom! It got bigger, and bigger, and.......

Between the older text (1921-1950, from the first and sixth editions) and the newer (1976) Norton science encyclopedia, it was obvious that science was much more straightforward in the pre-National Security Act days, and that in the newer text, there was a reflection of the fishy

88

attempts, brought on by the national security laws and the firmer establishment of the RQMs, to conceal certain scientific knowledge which had been discovered all the way back in 1912 by Langmuir. Aside from the discrepancies between older measurements, regarding the comparable outputs between the combustion of gasoline and the combustion of molecular hydrogen, and the output from the atomic hydrogen process, to the newer text, there was a failure, so far as I could determine, to state under appropriate references (or any others I could find), some important facts concerning atomic hydrogen, and even misrepresentations of the actual comparative outputs of gasoline and hydrogen combustion, through gobbledegook---the "badge of fraud"--- of which I spoke in *Space Aliens*. Norton apparently was forced by circumstances to rely on some 'scientists' who represented the fossil fuel cartels and other conflicting interests, while the older text was relatively free of such influences.

For example, in the newer text, at page 1311, energy from the combustion of hydrogen was stated at 29,000 calories per gram (52,200 BTU/lb). In the older text, this value was given at 62,100 BTU per pound of hydrogen, with a comparative value for gasoline ("petroleum") at 19,800 BTU per pound (stretched to 20,825 BTU per pound in the newer encyclopedia). These figures roughly comported with those in the encyclopedia for n-Heptane ("gasoline") at 19,314 BTU/lb, and hydrogen at 51,571.4 BTU/lb, which are more or less repeated at page 1137, with n-Heptane at 10,737.2 cal./gram, and Hydrogen at 28,669.6 cal./gram, yet nowhere in the newer text was the total output from atomic hydrogen given that I could find, and nowhere in the newer or older texts was it affirmatively stated that the hydrogen was not "consumed" in the process.

The corrected figure (52,200 BTU/lb) shows, in a comparison between the combustion of "normal hydrogen" (to form H_2O or water) and gasoline (to form CO_2), that hydrogen has a yield of roughly 2.7 times that of gasoline, by weight. Then we come to a comparison between gasoline and atomic hydrogen. Though the two can be compared BTU-for-BTU and pound-for-pound, showing atomic hydrogen's phenomenal output, the real measure of the atomic hydrogen process is gleaned only from a comparison between the "input energy"---103 cal./gram molecule---and the net output. The "input energy" would be "unity" for the process, because the process does not 'consume' the hydrogen, but only returns it to its associated state as H_2. The dissociation energy, subtracted from the gross output, would be the net output:

> 109,000 cal/gram mole (gross heat output)
> Minus - <u>103 cal/gram mole</u> (dissociation energy = "Unity")
> Leaves - 108,897 cal/gram mole (net output - "Over-Unity"
> because the hydrogen didn't have that
> much calorific energy in the first place,
> and was not 'consumed' in the second place)

In the atomic hydrogen process, hydrogen is not really a "fuel", but rather a "medium" used in the extraction of and conversion of energy from the ether, by transforming invisible radiation and electrical energy into infrared (heat) radiation. The energy required to pump the recombined hydrogen to a holding tank, before being recycled and shot back across the arc and into the reaction chamber once again, is not considered in this computation. This energy should be negligible, since the dissociation energy is barely more than a thousandth of the gross output, and there is probably a way to make the process work without a pump anyway.

The manipulators of information have both lied and made the direct comparison between atomic hydrogen and gasoline as difficult as possible, but I have waded through a multi-step mathematical, physical, chemical and unitary process to get to the truth. Atomic hydrogen produces over 109 k.cal./gram molecule, which is 109,000 k.cal./kilo. Minus the 103 cal./gram mole endothermic dissociation energy, and a net of 108,897 k.cal./kilo is left. A kilo equals 2.205 lbs., so a pound equals 453.51 grams. You must divide the net cal./kilo by lb./kilo to get cal./lb., then multiply this times °F/°C (1.8) to get °F/lb. This is then divided by grams/lb. to get <u>196,015</u> BTU/lb. The gross is <u>196,200 btu/lb.</u> In comparison to 19,314 BTU/lb for n-Heptane, atomic hydrogen has <u>10.5 times</u> the energy per pound (of H_1 per gal. of H_2O). There is an easier mathematical process, but this shows more clearly what I did.

No wonder the process "went out of use". With this process, a home consumer would pay nothing for fuel, because he could produce a small amount of hydrogen in his basement, any time he needed it, and could use it over and over, *ad infinitum*. He could heat his house, drive his car, and use it for "home-industrial" uses. In a motor cruiser on the ocean, one would never have to worry about where the "next gallon" of fuel was coming from, or what it would "cost", because like sunshine, the heat from atomic hydrogen is "free", except, unlike sunshine, you could produce as much as you want, any time, day or night, summer or winter, rain or shine; the farmer would no longer be dependent upon the oil cartels for his energy, and could run his machinery and heat his barns "free". He could tell the fuel suppliers and the banks to screw themselves. People in the far Alaskan north could heat large spaces without huge expense. "Northern industry" would thrive again. The population control Nazis will hate me.

It is obvious that the reason corporations like ARCO went so heavily into producing solar energy equipment in the early '70s, was so they could control and ultimately raise the cost of (free) solar energy, to make it "competitive" with gasoline and other fossil fuels.

There are many ways used in contemporary texts to confuse facts, but the most effective way is by complete omission. Such facts could not have been concealed by "accident" or mere "oversight", because they are too phenomenal. Only by plowing through a tortuous mathematical process and confusing units and other factors was the true motive for such concealment revealed for certain, but tell me why I'm not surprised?

Conservatively speaking, the atomic hydrogen process bears a 10.5-to-1 ratio to n-Heptane. Would you care for 315 miles per gallon? How about 550,000 miles? It all depends on how many times you recycle it.

The figures for n-Heptane are grossly confusing, as one might expect, since it is shown only by comparison by weight that hydrogen combustion has a 2.7-to-1 ratio to n-Heptane. This deception was effected by playing around with differing heat and weight units, pressures, and volumes, and the difference between the centigrade and Fahrenheit scales. The "109,000 cal./gram molecule" figure for atomic hydrogen was omitted from the newer text , though one might have been able to extrapolate it from some complex data stated in other areas where the inquisitive person is not expected to look. There was a total absence in the new text or other "new" data available to me, of a direct comparison of energy outputs between combustion of petroleum and hydrogen, much less the atomic hydrogen process.

I have never seen a direct comparison by any of the thousands of Ph.D.s in chemistry or physics, who should have become aware of these facts during their cursory studies. To make these figures even more ludicrous, with BTU ("British Thermal Units"), one would expect the weight to be shown in kilos under the metric system, instead of the nonmetric "pounds". These machinations clearly appear to rely upon the well-founded assumption that all scientists who know, are controlled and don't say, and those who aren't controlled, will be considered "quacks" if they <u>try</u> to say. Again, its the usual case of "Those who know, can't say, and those who say, will be presumed not to know."

Another stupid trick used is to compare "system weights", under the false assumption that the user of hydrogen would have to use only the systems <u>they</u> present, raising the "comparable" weight of hydrogen to gasoline, using cumbersome cryogenic bottles or hydride storage tanks, etc., when the simple figures clearly show that one-third the amount by weight of hydrogen would be needed for a comparable combustion process. Whenever hydride systems are mentioned, there is an obvious omission of the *liquid* hydride system developed by Dr. Gerald Schafflander of California, the promotion for which Schafflander and associates were abusively prosecuted by the SEC, as previously stated in *Space Aliens*. Yet, the atomic hydrogen process would be more than adequate---even fantastic---with only a pound of hydrogen, and one could carry an extra 25 lbs of Dr. Schafflander's liquid hydride in the trunk. Below is a direct comparison between the BTU/lb for combustion of gasoline and molecular hydrogen, and the atomic hydrogen process, respectively:

Gasoline combustion (n-Heptane)	19,314 BTU/lb
Hydrogen combustion ($H_2 + O$)	52,200 BTU/lb
Atomic hydrogen ($H_2 \rightleftharpoons 2H$)	196,200 BTU/lb

Note that the atomic hydrogen process does not involve a "consumption" of the hydrogen, yet even if it did, the ratio between atomic hydrogen and gasoline is still 10.5-to-one. Take into consideration also that all the best methods for obtaining over a hundred miles per gallon (even *hundreds* of miles per gallon) of gasoline in automobile engines, utilize the vaporization of gasoline and mixture of it with air prior to combustion, something which is easier to do with hydrogen, because it is in a *gaseous* state at normal temperatures and pressures. Also consider that while n-Heptane is a 'purer' gasoline, it hasn't been available for years, and most "gasoline" is a dilute mixture with water and various additives, with only about 50% n-Heptane, so I'm being as kind as I can be to "gasoline".

If a pound of gasoline could propel a car 30 miles, the consumption would be 666.6 BTU/mile. On the same scale, a pound of atomic hydrogen would yield 315 miles. Then you could repeat it, over and over and over. A pound of hydrogen could conceivably supply all your energy needs for your whole life, and you could produce another 100 pounds of it electrolytically, right in your basement, from tap water! Is this free energy, or what?!

Though the facts of this "secret" hydrogen process are "hidden in plain sight", one must beware of the disinformation, as well as the common mistakes created by "scientists" who have been duped by the RQMs. For example, in the 1976 Norton Encyclopedia, 5th Edition, page 1311, most of the pertinent facts about hydrogen are shown. The "109,000 cal./gram molecule" for recombined hydrogen, reported in an older text, was not shown directly, though the following facts which *were* shown, are of particular note:

Heat of vaporization at 20.4°K	107	cal/gram
Energy released upon combustion	29,000	cal/gram
Heat of combustion at 25°C	63,317.4	cal/gram mole - gross
Heat of combustion at 25°C	57,797.6	cal/gram mole - net

ANOTHER ASTOUNDING PROOF AND MORE HYDROGEN METHODS

The Norton encyclopedia was in its 5th edition, and the "103 cal./gram mole" dissociation energy did not appear to be a typo or misprint, and should have been corrected by that time if discovered. How many books would I have to search to find such a 'misprint', especially since I didn't expect to find the anomaly because of the obvious concealment? Yet, in *Physical Chemistry* (1965) by E. A. Moelwyn-Hughes of Cambridge (Pergamon Press, London), at page 418, appeared the following:

"The Spectroscopic evaluation of the dissociation energy

The energy of dissociation, D_e, of a diatomic molecule is the difference between the potential energy of the atoms when infinitely separated, and their energy when the atoms are at rest at the equilibrium separation."

Notice that the "at rest" state of the *molecules*, is couched in language that makes you think that the "infinitely separated" atomic hydrogen *atoms* represents the "excited state" for the *element*. In layman's terms, the RQMs simply made the statement that the dissociation and recombination energies *had* to be the same, because their theories depended upon them being the same. Then they measured the dissociation energy backwards, by measuring the recombination energy, and stating the measurement *as if it were* the dissociation energy. The statements are supplanted by a lot of RQM gobbledegook, with a "spectroscopic evaluation" thrown in like some snake oil, because the spectroscope purportedly "can't lie". There is also in the same text, at page 417, the following obtuse statement:

"...In kilocalories per mole, D_e is 109."

If hydrogen atoms exothermically release energy when they combine to form molecules, the potential energy has been lost by the molecules, yet they attribute the "potential energy" to the hydrogen *molecules*---backwards---to evade their duty to draw the logical conclusion. This lie is shown by a graph ("fig. 4") purporting to show the "potential energy of the hydrogen *molecule* in the *ground electronic state*." This clearly misrepresents, by a Ph.D. in physics of the "Royal Society", that hydrogen in the "atomic state" is not in a ground state, but in an excited state. In this 1965 physical chemistry text from England, the heat energy generated on recombination of the hydrogen atom is given as 109,000 cal./gram mole, then misrepresented as the "potential energy" of the "ground state hydrogen molecules" which have just formed! But the "ground state" of hydrogen is the atomic state, with the electron at its *lowest level of energy*, so the RQMs are hoist by their own petards, since there is no way the ground state atoms could "store" the 109,000 cal./gram molecule. Where, exactly would this energy "reside"? Concurrently, this same figure is falsely equated with the heat generated exothermally when two hydrogen atoms---each in its "excited state"---come together to form a molecule. Since the heat energy is released on recombination, the molecules lack the potential energy already released. The potential energy of the separate atoms in their ground states, is greater than that of the molecules, because the heat energy is released from the entrained ether and converted ZPR---not from the hydrogen *atoms*---when they combine to form molecules.

94

This is hereby unmasked as Orwellian <u>doublethink</u>. Since when is the potential energy of the atom of an element measured from its molecular state? This is exactly like saying that a truck sitting at the bottom of a hill has more "potential energy" than one sitting at the top, because of the energy required to drive it up to the top of the hill! What a strange way to define "potential energy". It is like saying an empty gas can has the potential energy of the gas that it takes to fill it up!

The unique thing about the hydrogen atom, is that it is "born" at the top of the hill! Its astounding properties lie in its ability to perform as a "doorway" between the ether and the world of more familiar atomic matter.

The relativist statements have been unwittingly accepted as correct, because there is no ether or Zero Point Radiation possible under their theories, and the molecules have to have more energy than the atoms separately, because "$E = MC^2$". The RQMs have misrepresented and concealed this process in which separate atoms---with lower *MASS*---possess more "atomic" energy than the molecules! Ha! These facts on hydrogen show that E equals <u>*M U C H   M O R E   T H A N*</u> MC^2.

Under relativism and quantum mechanics, "solid" matter is thought erroneously to be the most "compact", "stored" form of "atomic energy", because the energy is supposed to be released by the "smashing" and destruction, or fusing together of atoms, which Tesla said was false. It is clearly shown by the atomic hydrogen reaction that Tesla was right and the relativists and Einstein were wrong, because the hydrogen atoms have more potential energy in a separate atomic state than they do in the diatomic molecular state! This can only be either because when separate, the atoms "gather" energy from the ZPR, and eject it from the ether when recombined! In either case, the energy is not stored by the atoms, and no longer possessed by the molecules after release, unless there is an even greater lie hiding in the relativist bushes.

This perverse potential energy fallacy is also a way to confuse the diatomic hydrogen *molecules* with the nascent atomic hydrogen *atoms* produced by the hydrolysis of water. The energy of hydrolysis is equated with the energy of dissociation, and the energy of combustion with the energy of recombination, yet the information presented here shows that by combining the hydrolysis of water, in which atomic hydrogen is produced directly, with the atomic hydrogen recombination process, instead of the combustion process---and perhaps throwing the oxygen away---that at least <u>10.5</u> times as much energy as the hydrolytic input

95

can be produced, in still a third astounding hydrogen free energy process. This is true because the atomic hydrogen process without question releases at least 3.75 times the BTUs by weight, as ordinary hydrogen does in the combustion process. Even the relativists agree that the "energy of combustion" equals at least the "energy of hydrolysis" (even though it is well known that the industrial production of hydrogen by electrolysis is generally 120% efficient). Production of atomic hydrogen directly by hydrolysis, which cuts out a separate dissociation operation, is yet another exciting possibility. It does not expend the electrical equivalent of 109,000 cal./gram molecule (to produce only 65 cubic centimeters of hydrogen gas).

HOW DOES IT WORK?

As a "welding process", this process was 'obsolesced' by MIG and TIG welding, neither of which can compare to its welding efficiency and uses. Since the welding process was its only "public" use in the years past, the "new" processes allowed industry to toss the "obsolete" process onto the junk heap (except for their own 'secret' use of it). The "new" processes were promoted by U-Know-Who, motivating their welding suppliers and the electric power companies at their own levels. More archaic tanks, transformers, gauges, torches, electrodes, gases, fluxes, and electric power, etc., etc., to be sold at a hefty profit. If people generate their own hydrogen for welding at home, how much equipment, supplies and power will they buy?

How does the atomic hydrogen obtain its energy, if not from the "ether"? No wonder establishment science doesn't want you to know there is an ether. If we are to believe the "law of conservation of energy", as interpreted by establishment (relativistic, ether-excluding) 'science', this process is impossible, yet using data available from 'standard' texts, I have shown that the input energy of 103 cal./gram molecule is somehow either 'magnified' to 109,000 cal./gram molecule of hydrogen---a multiplication of over 1,058 times---or that, by use of hydrogen as a "medium", that the 103 calories is 'seed' energy (called the "activation energy"), triggering the atomic hydrogen's apprehension of a net 108,897 cal./gram molecule, from the "ether".

An equally phenomenal "atomic helium" process (reported in *Space Aliens*) is 4.6 times this output. It can be conducted the same way, and produces the same kind of electrical energy and radiation-to-heat energy

96

transformation, in which "mass" is only a "medium" used in the process. The same principles are shared by the Atomic Hydrogen Process, by Josef Papp's *Method and Means of Converting Atomic Energy into Utilizable Kinetic Energy* (Patent No. 3,670,494, of June 20, 1972), and several other discoveries mentioned here. If these processes used as much electrical energy as they produced, and electrical energy was the end product sought, what would be the use of the processes, right? At the comparable 30 mpg for n-Heptane, helium could produce 42.86 times as much, or about 1285.8 miles per pound.

According to *Van Nostrand's Scientific Encyclopedia*, 5th ed., Van Nostrand Reinhold Co. (1976), simple electron bombardment of helium gas, in a special chamber, excites the helium atom to a temporarily radioactive isotope of extremely short half-life. In this state, the helium atom unpairs its electrons, promotes one electron to the 2s state (in which state it remains for only a very short time), and afterward releases 460,000 cal/gram-atom (per gram of helium), on collapse of the excited atom back to its ground state. The heat is in the form of photons. This is similar to the process for atomic hydrogen, as illustrated by my drawing shown on page 102. It is my theory that while the electron clouds are in the excited (expanded) state, they gather and convert energy from the ZPR.

Apparently, as the hydrogen passes through the arc, the electric and magnetic fields, plus heat, provide the activation energy triggering the molecule's 'apprehension' of an additional 108,897 cal./gram molecule of endothermic dissociation energy. Just exactly could this be possible? Since each hydrogen atom is composed of a proton and an electron (each with a pair of purportedly equal and opposite charges) one would expect the binding force between the molecules to be very weak, but when the atoms are separated they purportedly expand greatly in size---because negative ions are larger than the non-metal atoms from which they are formed---encompassing a greater <u>volume</u> of *Omni Matter* (my term for the "ether"). On recombination, the atoms shrink in volume, as the excess 'gathered' energy is squeezed out of the ether as free (heat) energy. The "endothermic" dissociation absorbs only 103 cal/gram molecule, yet on recombination, the atoms "exothermically" yield a net 108,897 cal/gram molecule. How exactly does this occur?

As stated in *Space Aliens*, it is my theory that all space is packed solid with bumper-to-bumper "Omni Particles" (A.K.A., "the ether"). This elusive yet dense and ultra fine, absolutely transparent matter, is meanwhile being omnidirectionally interpenetrated by something called Zero Point Radiation ("ZPR"), of such high frequency and voltage, that it is difficult to measure or comprehend. This radiation is in (non-relativistic) equilibrium, therefore referred to as "Zero Point" radiation.

The facts proven by the atomic hydrogen process, explained by the involvement of the Omni Matter and the ZPR, are forbidden by relativity and quantum mechanics, in which a simple harmonic oscillator cannot have a stationary state of zero <u>kinetic</u> energy, because the ground state still has one half quantum of energy and the appropriate motion, yet by relativity's 'other' rules, the principles of kinetic energy has no applicability to electromagnetic radiation (the ZPR). Since relativity also rejects the existence of an ether, there is nothing in so-called "empty space" to contain such radiant energy, and the atomic hydrogen process would have to create its energy from "nothing", therefore violating the law of conservation of energy, as misinterpreted by the relativists, who see all energy functions as part of the 'winding down' products of an "original" BIG BANG.

You can forget what the relativists said. The equilibrium of the ZPR can be upset by disturbances created in the Omni Matter---which I divide into Omnions (ultra-fine, positive "subprotonic" particles) and Omnitrons ("sub-electronic" charges carried by the Omnions---all of which the ZPR interpenetrates. Unidirectional vibrations (disturbances) in the Omni Matter cause it to accumulate transferred force from the ZPR, throwing Omni Matter out of equilibrium, and restoring equilibrium to the ZPR. The Omni Matter's excess force is then transferred through the atomic hydrogen atoms (or other temporarily excited, enlarged atoms encompassing it) into the atomic mass frequencies, during disturbance, thus restoring equilibrium to the Omni Matter. This transferred force is not "energy created from nothing", but only represents a change in the "form" of some of the infinite energy (force over time), already existing in 'space' in other forms (such as the ZPR, or as "sub-electronic" charges).

Whenever H_2 is dissociated to 2H (H), and the single electron clouds enlarge to encompass more Omni Matter (affected by a greater ZPR), there is a reaction with and transfer of force from exothermic atomic sources, through the molecules, into stripped Omnions which were entrapped to bind the atoms together. This exothermic energy is sufficient to throw the Omnions within the electron clouds, and concentrated in the space between the atoms, beyond their electronic

98

quantum boundaries, so that the additional energy needed to dissociate the atoms is regained from the surrounding Omni Matter and ZPR, restoring the equilibrium of the Omni Matter. With the recombination of the atomic hydrogen to form 2H, the converted ZPR radiant energy, and sub-electronic charges---which I call Omnitrons---is ejected (squeezed out) from the atoms, as heat or other interconverted radiant energy of lower frequency, as the electron clouds shrink with the addition of positive charge carried by the Omnions. The reason the electron cloud density of the hydrogen molecule is more concentrated in the area around the space between the atoms, is because of the entrained Omnions' presence there. Otherwise, the two negative charges carried by the two atoms would cause mutual repulsion. Actually, since heat is infrared-spectrum radiation, the process can be conceived as a means of converting the ZPR from an ultra-penetrating positive ('cold') spectrum radiation, to a mass-reactive infrared (heat) spectrum radiation, and that is the proximate "source" of the so-called "free energy", in the form of exothermic heat radiation. The ZPR is an analog to sunshine, except it penetrates all matter all the time and is not affected by day or night, so it can be converted to usable energy all the time with the appropriate technology, such as the atomic hydrogen process.

Incidentally, this same atomic hydrogen process, as first published here and now, is also the apparent source of the anomalous exothermic heat produced in aqueous cavitation, as well as in the so-called "cold fusion" process, which are two other free energy processes which are based on the atomic hydrogen process. In addition, it is the phenomenon which was apparently responsible for the cavitation-based, powerful fuelless pumping action produced by the "Hydro Vacuo Motor" of John Ernst Worrell Keely, in c. 1870..

The atomic hydrogen atoms have single, unpaired electrons in enlarged shells. These atoms are in Mendeleev's Group I-a, and all the atoms in that group have unpaired outer electrons, and are photo-reactive to and transmute when exposed to ultraviolet light, as do all the atoms of elements below atomic number 19. Some of these elements transmute in visible and infrared light, and all of them can be used to transmute ZPR into usable free energy. This photo-reactivity creates temporary, artificial-radioactivity-producing isotopes of short half-life, with the emission of photon energy restoring equilibrium to the atoms as they return to their ground states. The energy for these radioactive emissions comes from the ether, not from the atoms themselves. The atoms can be analogized by certain crystals, described by the *Raman Effect*, in which light passing through the crystals is "stepped down" to lower frequencies. The infrared spectrum light produced by the atomic hydrogen process is thermally reactive with normal atomic and molecular matter, because of its longer wavelengths.

The transfer of force from the ZPR, via the Omni Matter, through the dissociated H_1 atoms, is apparently the kind of thing somewhat cryptically spoken of by Tesla, when he stated: "There is no energy in matter other than that received from the environment."[4.]

In so-called "cold fusion", the electrolytic cell produces "nascent hydrogen", just like in the atomic hydrogen process, and the recombination of the monoatomic hydrogen to 2H releases heat, the product claimed. This atomic hydrogen process also proves Tesla's theory that "atomic energy" comes from the environment, not from 'smashing' atoms. It proves that "mass" does not even enter into the equation, and that Einstein's "$E = MC^2$" is <u>wrong</u>. Einstein's theory says this process as I describe it could only be possible if the hydrogen were 'annihilated', converting its "mass" into heat, and otherwise, is impossible. But the hydrogen is still hydrogen, before, during, and after the process, and Einstein was wrong, wrong, wrong! It defies relativism, Heisenberg's "uncertainty" principle, misinterpreted quantum mechanics, and the BIG BANG!

Perhaps this or a similar process was also what Leland Anderson referred to in his eulogy of Tesla, when he mentioned his "plucking" thermal units "...right out of the thin air". After all, the hydrogen atoms when in the 2H molecular form are smaller, therefore "compressed". Compression of a gas releases heat radiation, usually thought to originate with the energy endothermically absorbed during decompression, but in the case of hydrogen, the change is effected by the natural, physical process of recombination to 2H. The molecular atoms can be 'decompressed' by a slight application of heat of dissociation, because the strong binding force between the atoms created by the Omnions, is more easily weakened by a small amount of exothermic energy sufficient to separate the atoms, so that the Omnions regain their Omnitronic charges from the surrounding ether and ZPR. Hydrogen atoms have the highest charge-to-mass ratio known, a ratio which almost completely neutralizes the protons. 'Decompression' of the electron clouds occur during dissociation, because there is less positive mass within the clouds to pull the clouds down toward the protons. As the protons dissociate with application of the 103 cal/gram molecule, this allows the greatly expanded electron clouds of the atoms to encompass a larger volume or Omnions, carrying sub-electronic Omnitronic charges equal to 108,897 cal/gram molecule, from the only source available, the ZPR and Omni Matter (A.K.A., "ether"). Since there is no great cooling activity in the proximate area of dissociation, the 'heat' can only come from the Omni Matter and ZPR, and is ultimately a <u>conversion</u> of energy in the form of random, 'cold' ZPR, and Omnitronic charges, into a coherent, utilizable form of heat radiation. This process, though it can be thermally triggered, is not merely a thermal process, because the net energy released is not converted originally from thermal energy, but from ZPR and Omnitrons, into infrared (thermal) radiation.

Amazingly, the raw data for this process came from ordinary science books, though the oldest text was produced in England, and would be practically unavailable to the average American experimenter. The full magnitude and output comparable to petroleum was only obviated by conversion of weights, measures, units and temperature scales, into a consistent picture, to obtain the total net outputs. Most physicist or chemists would refuse to believe the results, even if they had calculated them themselves, and would insist that they had erred. This is indeed an inverted BIG LIE, which is told very <u>small</u>, and often. The BIG LIE consists of a denial that there is an ether, the distortion of quantum mechanics, and the exaggeration and minimalization of other incompatible measurements, to create a false overall picture. This is then backed up by a vacuum of information, in publicly available texts and other sources, created via the National Security Act, by the Fuel/Power Cartels.

APPROPRIATE USE OF THE PROCESS

Now that we are beginning to understand our atomic-hydrogen, free energy system, and the great magnitude of its output, what are its most appropriate and immediately applicable uses?

The most direct, appropriate use of this technology appears to be to provide heat for homes, as well as for home-industrial heating purposes, such as in agriculture. A secondary use would be to produce heat for steam to drive turbine-powered electric generators, or for motive power for cars, trucks, boats, trains and planes. This system would be excellent if coupled with a refrigerant-driven, closed-loop turbo-electric generator, to provide electric power for electro-propulsive flying saucers, the ultimate in private transportation.

Since the net output is heat, the first order of business is a special heat exchanger, to transfer heat to water or other media, or to produce steam for turbine power. The heat in the reaction chamber of the atomic hydrogen furnace must be quickly removed by the exchanger to prevent a buildup of heat sufficient to melt the reactor surfaces which receive and catalyze the recombining gas atoms. The simplified design shown below is merely a proposal.

Years ago, German metallurgists developed a hydrogen furnace which used a copper crucible in a closed system which created the "hydrogen environment" required for reduction of the platinum group compounds. To withstand the high temperatures required for the reductions, the copper crucible was cooled from below by water, which removed the heat fast enough to prevent melting of the copper, as platinum metals were melted in it with the torch from above. The occlusion of oxygen prevented oxidation of the crucible and the platinum metals, and insured reduction of the platinum compounds by the hydrogen. This idea, together with over 45 years familiarity and use of pyro-technology and over 34 years of welding, has influenced the design of this (simplified version) atomic hydrogen furnace:

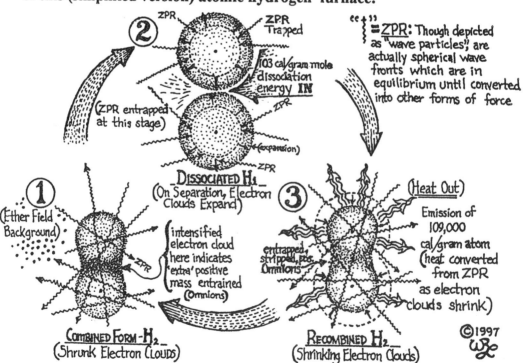

102

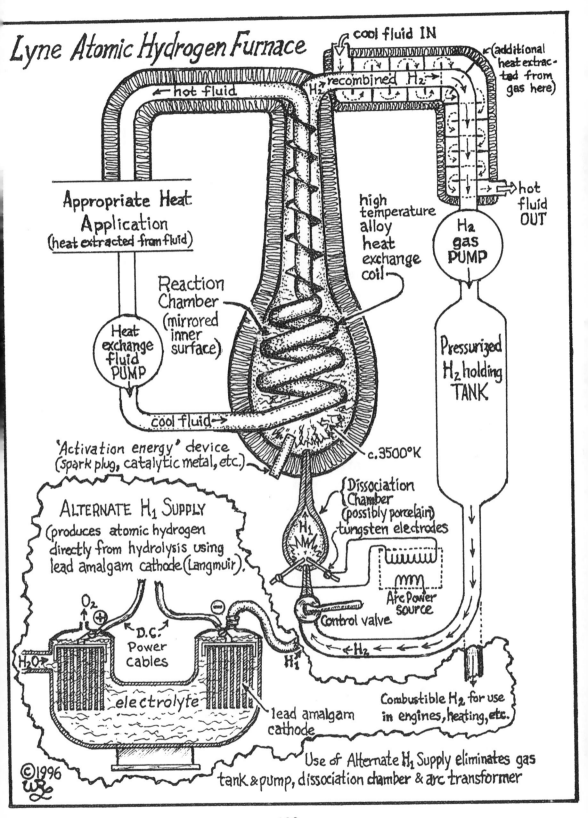

Lyne Atomic Hydrogen Furnace

cool fluid IN

← hot fluid

H₂ recombined H₂

k (additional heat extracted from gas here)

hot fluid OUT

H₂ gas PUMP

Appropriate Heat Application
(heat extracted from fluid)

high temperature alloy heat exchange coil

Heat exchange fluid PUMP

Reaction Chamber
(mirrored inner surface)

Pressurized H₂ holding TANK

cool fluid →

'Activation energy' device
(spark plug, catalytic metal, etc.)

c. 3500°K

Dissociation Chamber
(possibly porcelain)
tungsten electrodes

ALTERNATE H₁ SUPPLY
(produces atomic hydrogen directly from hydrolysis using lead amalgam cathode (Langmuir).

H₁

Arc Power Source

O₂ ↑ +

D.C. Power cables

⊖

H₂O →

Control valve

← H₂ ←

H₁

electrolyte

lead amalgam cathode

Combustible H₂ for use in engines, heating, etc.

© 1996
WL

Use of Alternate H₁ Supply eliminates gas tank & pump, dissociation chamber & arc transformer

FREE ENERGY SURPRISE
Ether, ZPR & "Environmental" Energy

The following concerns a device which appears to unequivocally disproves Einstein's relativity theories and proves Nikola Tesla's nuclear theories.

Based on material in *Space Aliens* (pgs. vii, 185 and 187), a researcher invited me to collaborate in a 50/50 development of a device (similar to that shown on page vii), with the provision that I not use his name. I suggested using an iron pipe and 15 kv transformer, based on Tesla's use of an iron "antenna" in a Colorado Springs experiment. With an approx. .1 amp/120 volt input (12 watts), an output of 48 kw was achieved. Since the K-capture level of iron is 7,110 volts, I suggested tuning the two 7,500-volt legs to 7,110 with a variac (total voltage 14,220), at which the output jumped to 66 kw, a gain of over 38%.

With 120 v/.1 amps/60 cps/14.22 kv going into the <u>ungrounded</u> device, the output (on the same leads) is apparently superimposed at high frequency, so that, while maintaining the high voltage 'excitation electric field', the output can be extracted by high voltage high frequency filter and rectifier, thence reduced to usable electric power with an inverter.

In "K-capture", the innermost "K-orbit" electron of iron drops into the nucleus, converting a proton into an extra neutron. This appears to render the iron unstable (i.e., "radioactive" in the Tesla sense), so that it disturbs the equilibrium of and reacts with the ZPR, converting some of it into an electrical output, via the iron. This device has also been said to transmute zinc to mercury, when used in a different way to produce great heat. At this point in time the device is somewhat of an enigma, which appears to produce great energy.

As the device runs it hums, with no arcing, as a cool shaft of air exits its top, with strong electric/magnetic fields about it. Some ozone appears to be forming. This was probably (part of) what Tesla meant when he said "I have a new use for iron", and "...it is when things are quiet that something is really going on".

For a copy of *Free Energy Surprise* (© 1997, William R. Lyne,), a set of plans and documentary photos send $10. (including postage) to: Creatopia Productions, General Delivery, Lamy, New Mexico 87540; Tel/Fax (505) 466-3022.

CONCLUSION

<u>196,200</u> <u>BTUs</u> is a lot of energy from a pound of hydrogen. I have to pinch myself. Then repeat it 10,000 times.

When this kind of "atomic energy" hit a small segment of the unknowing American public---the welders---in the late '40s, there were newspaper stories saying that the trans-Atlantic voyages of the Queen Mary could be powered by a hunk of radioactive material the size of a golf ball. They told their exaggerated stories that way when they wanted us to get hooked and pay for it, but today's "nuclear reactors" produce electricity at the same efficiency level as coal and gas-fired generators (38%), and we still have to deal with the inevitable problems of greater expense, entrenched, archaic, stagnant "nuclear" and fossil fuel technology, nuclear decay, waste, and probable devastation ala *Cernobyl*.

The stumbling blocks to the use of hydrogen are actually illusions, created by the corporate-state coercive monopolists---*CommuNazis (A.K.A., IllumiNazis)*. The atomic hydrogen process was discovered in 1912 by Langmuir, and was developed as a "welding process" in the '30s. The DOE 'scientists' at Los Alamos said the use of hydrogen involves heavy, cumbersome cryogenic tanks and equipment, until a liquid hydride system developed by Dr. Gerald Schafflander of California, was pointed out by me, in a letter to the New Mexican in 1980, totally ridiculing their phony efforts in 1979. Then Schafflander and associates were prosecuted by the SEC, because the liquid hydride stored hydrogen in something like "rock salt"---which cracked out at about 70° C. DOE scientists mention only the heavier, more cumbersome, solid metallic hydride systems. Schafflander's lighter liquid hydride system, which uses solar-voltaics to generate the hydrogen, would be a wonderful way to store and deliver hydrogen for the atomic hydrogen process. Goodbye, oil cartels, hello atomic hydrogen, it's pay-back time!

By the way, the reason my "cold fusion" process (using my weird, <u>lead</u>-based cathode) which I tested back in 1980, worked so well (<u>see</u> *Space Aliens from the Pentagon* [5.], pg. 198), was because Langmuir, back in 1912, said a <u>lead amalgam</u> cathode produced "nascent (atomic) hydrogen". Cold fusionists, throw away your palladium cathodes and get lead amalgam! Watch the price of water rise to $1.40 per gallon. After all, why should "they" allow "us" to buy a whole gallon of pure H_2O "chemicals" for less, especially when a gallon is enough for a lifetime?

References:

1. J. R. Partington (Emeritus Prof. Of Chem., Univ. Of London), A Text-Book of Inorganic Chemistry, (Sixth Edition, 1953), Macmillan & Co. Ltd., London

2. Van Nostrand's Scientific Encyclopedia, Fifth Edition (Edited by Douglas M. Considine), Van Nostrand Reinhold Company (1976)

3. E. A. Moelwyn-Hughes, Physical Chemistry (Second Revised Edition), Pergamon Press, London (1965)

4. Nikola Tesla, Lecture Before the Institute of Immigrant Welfare, May 12, 1938

5. William R. Lyne, Space Aliens From the Pentagon, (First Edition, 1993; Second Edition, 1995), Creatopia Productions, General Delivery, Lamy, New Mexico 87540

William Lyne was born in Big Spring, Texas in 1938 and raised in west Texas oil boom towns, two years in the Bay Area of northern California during WW II, and the southeast Texas Big Thicket country. He has a B.S. in Fine Arts and Industrial Arts (1965) from Sam Houston State University, Huntsville, Texas, and an M.F.A. in Studio Arts (1969) from the University of Texas at Austin. He has been living in New Mexico for the past 27 years, and resides just to the south of Santa Fe, in the little railroad town of Lamy, with his 13-year-old son Angus.

In 1993, he published *Space Aliens From the Pentagon: Flying Saucers are Man-Made Electrical Machines.* In 1995, a revised and expanded second edition of this book was issued. The result has been the illegal dissemination of a vast quantity of false government propaganda, via covert intelligence agents in the "UFOlogy" community, to overcome the effects of the book.